SEXY LIBERAL!

OF ME I SING

by Stephanie Miller

Gival Press

D1570371

Arlington, Virgi

For information:
Stephanie Miller
 c/o David Black Agency
335 Adams Street
Brooklyn, NY 11201
www.stephaniemiller.com

Published by Gival Press, an imprint of Gival Press, LLC.
For information:
Gival Press, LLC
P. O. Box 3812
Arlington, VA 22203
www.givalpress.com

First paperback edition ISBN: 978-1-940724-06-5
Library of Congress Control Number: 2016939864

Cover artwork: © by Ross Bigley.
Book design by Ken Schellenberg.

CONTENTS

DEDICATION

This book is dedicated to my Dad, who left us too soon, but who I would rather have had as a daddy for the 21 years I had him, than any other daddy for a lifetime.

And to my Mom, who is equally wonder-ful, and still around to be horrified by this book, and yet I imagine, oddly proud, as usual. I love you, Mom. Sorry about all the swear words.

IT'S ALL
ABOUT ME

There are a few things you need to know about me right up front.

If you're offended by crass, tasteless, scatological humor, scrawled on a Chardonnay-soaked cocktail napkin, then bite me, you oversensitive prude. If not, step up to the bar, baby! You've got my number. Tell Mama all of your problems… and I'll definitely make them far, far worse. I'm like a liberal Dr. Laura (if you can imagine that) or a filthy Dr. Oz, and, trust me, I'm highly qualified to give you horrible advice based solely on my own disastrous life decisions.

And that happy-clappy place where you get to bring all of your worries, concerns, and conspiracy theories is my daily morning radio (and simulcast television) program, "The Stephanie Miller Show," a left-leaning political "Morning Zoo," a potty-mouthed PBS "Newshour," "Face the Nation" with erection parody songs, and more flatulent sound effects than you'll hear on a kindergarten playground. Instead of just more endless blather about Kim Kardashian and Kanye West (although the president is right, he is a jackass), we also revel in the comic gift that is Ted Cruz. I'm no expert in these matters. I didn't attend Georgetown Law or Harvard's Kennedy School. My degree from USC (the University for Spoiled Children) is in Theater Arts. But if, as it's said, Washington is like Hollywood for ugly people, then I am probably more qualified to talk politics than that florist Michael Savage, with his PhD in fucking botany. And, trust me, my naked pictures are MUCH better than Dr. Laura's, with her degree in *biology*, who once called gay people "biological mistakes." Hey Dr. L, maybe you can use white-out to correct the errors in THIS lesbionic biological mistake's book! AutoCorrect THIS, Dr. Buzzkill!

I ended up naming the show after myself because Ellen DeGeneres threatened to sue me if I called it "Ellen." Anyone who thinks that bitch is *nice* has never received a cease and desist order from her. Now I'm stuck hosting it, or I'd have to find someone else named "Stephanie Miller" to take over for me. Now my mother's name, it's true, also happens to be Stephanie Miller, but as a 92-year-old lifelong Republican (and all-around fabulous mom), I can see her taking the show in a slightly less, as she would say, "blue" direction. Her principle catch phrase would be her ever present catch-all for, well…EVERYTHING I SAY… "Oh, dear." See also: "Oh, Stephie. Oh, dear. Why do you have to be so BLUE?"

My show also includes the only two men I can't live without, my Executive Producer (and hot boy toy) Chris Lavoie, and our Voice Deity extraordinaire, impressionist Jim Ward. For reasons which my alcohol-saturated brain can no longer recall, they are referred to as "The Mooks," and I refer to myself as "Mama"—possibly because, as I recall, with the one or two dry brain cells I have left, that I once said "Mama needs her medicine" on the air, referring to my well-known addiction to box wine, or as my listeners like to class it up…"cardboardeaux." It's not a drinking PROB-

LEM, as I say, it's a drinking SOLUTION. Don't harsh my box wine mellow "program" people. I've got 12 steps to my fridge for my next glass, and I WILL fucking cut a bitch who gets in my way. Just say'n.

(Photo courtesy of Stephanie Miller)

Doing a daily morning show, I'm forced go to bed at "Stupid O'Clock" in order to get up at "Insane O'Clock." All the things that happen during those theoretical hours of the day that normal people call "evening" are just abstract concepts to me. Here are some of the effects of my "lifestyle choice":

- I have never seen the moon.

- For me, the Early Bird special at Denny's is a late night snack.

- I've heard that a man named Fallon hosts a television program every night. Someone told me his first name is Conan, but I'm not sure. I've never seen it.

- My cocktail hour begins at 3 p.m. At least in Newfoundland, that's after dark. I take comfort in knowing that.

- There really *are* vampires. (As you'd
  expect: most of them work for Goldman
  Sachs, looting Japan's Nikkei Stock
  Exchange before the SEC even wakes up.)

- My dogs howl at the sun.

- I view invitations to events that begin after
  6 p.m. as just plain rude.

- "Midnight at the Oasis" is a song about
  me waking up to get a glass of water.

- Insomnia is nature's way of saying *you can
  sleep when you're dead.* (I don't know what
  that means. I'm tired. Leave me alone.)

Another bizarre fact you should know about me is that even
though I'm a proud liberal, Republicans love me. Don't ask
me why. It's clearly a "Fatal Attraction" thing for them,
which normally ends in me boiling their bunny, politically
speaking. But they keep trying. Whenever Republicans
call into my show they begin with "I'm a conservative, but
I still really enjoy you." I actually have a relationship with
Sean Hannity. We have this weird frenemy thing—we've
hugged in public, and whenever we see each other at radio
conferences he says, "Why *do* I like you?" In fact Sean regularly features me in his "Left Wing Hate Speech" segment.
I like to think of him as the boy in school who knocked the
books out of my hand. "Hi Sean!" sigh. Hair twirl. I once
told *Newsweek* once, "He is kind of a big hunk of stud meat
even if he is Satan." You know, both things could be true.
Rush Limbaugh has called me a "babe." To return the favor when Rush said, four days into his presidency, "I hope
Obama fails," I told Larry King, "I think we can all agree

Rush should be executed for treason." Strangely, he didn't get the joke. I don't know why these rightwing nutjobs love me so much. They're all men, so I'd say it was my ass—but radio really doesn't do it justice.

For years, I told my listeners that I always do my show completely naked. Just like when Orson Welles scared the shit out of everybody by faking a live broadcast of a Martian invasion in 1938, I take full advantage of radio's power to excite the listeners' imaginations with just the timbre of my voice and my soundboard of exotic flatulence effects. I began in this radio business right after college, long before you could find my face on your lap (I'm talkin' about your *computer*, perv), and I discovered that my listeners—especially my dick-driven listeners—found me sexy in their own ideologically special ways. My liberal fans would wank to me in Birkenstocks and a gray ponytail, dropping the farmers market veggies from my Earth-friendly canvas tote while imagining me bending over the hood of their Prius. (Porn-site search term: "Organic action.") Conservatives stroke it by picturing me draped in a hammer and sickle flag, my rivulets of shiny hair cascading in slow motion as I remove my red proletariat bandanna. (Porn-site search term: "Hot Commie.")

It's a shame that video killed the radio porn star...

When Al Gore invited me to simulcast my radio show on camera for Current TV a few years ago, he was worried that the very sight of my spin-class-toned naked body would dangerously raise the Earth's temperature, although he didn't put it exactly that way. Now I realize that broadcasting me naked might have hindered his sale of the network to Al Jazeera for $500 million. Hey, Al, for a piece of that money, I'd have worn a red, white, and blue burqa.

Oh, and about the title of this book, "Sexy Liberal!"—I often say there's "a Tea Party going on in my pants!" Those of you who've seen me live during the Sexy Liberal Comedy tour, along with my comedy buddies like John Fugelsang among others, have watched me take cellphone pictures of my hoo-ha right on stage and then throw the camera back into the audience (just kidding, Mom, I would NEVER do that.) OK, she saw me do it in Ashville, North Carolina, but she didn't get it. She also didn't get the teabagging demonstration.

Actual dialogue: Mom: "Stephie, what was the man doing to you onstage?" Me: "Um, nothing, mom, we were playing leap frog." Ironically, the same lie she told me when I once walked in on her and Dad in the 70's. Ah, a rare, lovely moment of bipartisan unity (somewhere, a bipartisan unicorn just farted glitter and a bipartisan angel got its wings).

By the way, it all must have worked. The Sexy Liberal Comedy Tour broke box office records across America and led to a live recording that became the first political comedy album to reach #1 on the comedy charts for iTunes, Amazon.com, and Billboard (Shameless plug—buy it now! Nothing subtle about MY whoring—Mama needs her box wine!).

The actual reason I shove a camera down my pants is that people desperately want proof that there really *is* a festive gathering going on down there. Maybe they're hoping to get invited to the party. Well, everyone's invited—and so are you! The thing about being *liberal* is that no matter your race, religion, sexual orientation, income level, you're always welcome in another liberal's pants. And, hey, I'll even go commando for *you*.

The phrase "Sexy Conservative!" just doesn't cut it. It's an oxymoron. Former Senator (and now Heritage Foundation president) Jim DeMint is angry about the rising American debt ceiling. At least that's what his fundraising letters say. The truth is he's really angry because his dick hasn't risen in years. And why should it? There's nothing erotic about screwing America.

Let's face it, conservatives just don't *like* sex. They'll never have the kind of throbbingly erotic experiences we sexy liberals celebrate, the memories of which will sustain me when I'm in a rest home pretending my catheter is a microphone. I hate to break it to those wild and crazy Tea Partiers, but there's a *reason* that the Village People never had a guy in a tri-corner hat. And just the *idea* of getting frisky with Ann Coulter is about as sexy as humping a department store mannequin—even for an elderly bitter, childless loser like me. When your nickname is "The Party of 'No,'" you've pretty much disqualified yourself from ever being called "sexy." Obstructionist is just a political science term for cock-block. No one is turned on by someone who just *lays* there and always says no. Right, Mrs. Boehner?

Whether it's immigration reform, gun control, or the budget deficit, there has to be a willingness to compromise, try new positions, demonstrate flexibility, communicate your needs, stay in there as long as it takes, and come together to reach an electrifying breakthrough. Only then can you achieve that ultimate high—a policy orgasm that leaves each of you fully satisfied and panting next to each other on either side of the aisle. Yes, big boy, GIVE me that amendment! Make me TAKE that rider! You know I WANT your emergency supplemental!!

Conservatives don't think that way. It's like what Rush once told Greta Van Susteren, "You know, compromise is portrayed as this wonderfully erudite and elite, superior form of existence. And too often what it means in Washington is that conservatives have to compromise their core in order to be considered nice people or what have you. I'm about defeating them, Greta, not compromising with them." That's not hot. Even his name sounds like a premature ejaculation.

I put it to you, if liberals *aren't* sexy, why does Viagra only come in BLUE?

The phrase "Sexy Liberal" has really caught on. Simply by putting those two words up on theater marquees across the country, we created the most successful comedy tour in America, selling out shows even in Red States and in markets where my show isn't carried. We were a hit in places where liberals usually have to pass each other on the street without making eye contact, so as not to wind up in one of Sheriff Joe Arpaio's rehabilitation centers. With our show, we did the impossible in live comedy—we turned conservative hecklers into liberal *helpers*. They shouted out "We LOVE you, Mama!" At first, I didn't even know how to *react* to that. I'm used to comedy clubs where some drunk guy yells, "You suck! Show us your tits!" Republican fans finish my punch lines like it's *The Rocky Horror Picture Show*. I say, "Speaker John..." and they all yell "BONER!" in unison. I say, "You know San Diego right wing radio host, Roger Hedgehog?" And they always shout "COCK!" And then I say, "Oh right, Roger Hedge*COCK*, I always get that wrong." It's a true bonding experience when you and your audience are doing dick jokes together.

We even had "Steph-heads"—people who saw the "Sexy Liberal!" show five, six, seven times. I was like Jerry Garcia—only with smaller boobs. Our fans drove from city to city—even flew thousands of miles—to see the highlight of our show, a sophisticated, subtle, and witty commentary on the fracturing of the Republicans brought on by the advent of the Tea Party. Taking our cue from actual protest signs such as "Tea Bag the Liberal Dems before they Tea Bag You," I had the courage to do what that wuss Paul Krugman never does: I make a guy dangle his (fully-covered) testicles over my face for our extremely popular on-stage teabagging demonstration. Listen, my producer had to show me what it was on the interwebs (safe search off, kids!)

I don't get out much, as I'll discuss in my poignant, yet pathetic next book: "I Will Die Alone and Be Eaten by My Dogs." I consider live teabagging a public service for other loser elderly shut-ins like me. Lawrence O'Donnell's field of expertise is tax policy; mine is testicles.

But "Sexy Liberal!" isn't *all* about me. Not hardly. We actually chose the name "Sexy Liberal" as a joke, to one-up Justin Timberlake. He took "sexy" back and we're taking "liberal" back from the haters and hucksters who think that Hawaii is a province of Kenya and that black people can't be president. We're making "liberal" a dirty word, but only in a GOOD WAY. Grrrrr. Insert disgusting motion with my tongue here.

When we say "Sexy Liberal" we aren't talking about *ourselves*, we're talking about you. Yes, YOU! Because *being* liberal *is* sexy. It means you're open-minded, empathetic, compassionate—and an easy lay.

I try to be all of those things. But it raises a lot of questions: How did I—a good, late-Boomer, upstate New York, Goldwater-Miller Catholic girl—how did I become a Democratic cheerleader? How did I—an aspiring comedian who only wanted to become the next Lily Tomlin or Carol Burnett—wind up talking politics with pundits and pols every day on the radio and television? How did the daughter of Congressman William Miller, former RNC Chairman and 1964 Republican vice presidential nominee, transform herself into a Sexy Liberal?

In this book, I'm going to bare my soul, and various other things, and we'll find out.

ABANDONED BY WOLVES, RAISED BY REPUBLICANS

In 1964, my father, Congressman William E. Miller of New York, was chosen as the Republican nominee for Vice President of the United States by Senator Barry Goldwater. Mostly, Dad's job was to start nearly every speech by saying, "What Barry *meant to say was...*"

(Photo courtesy of Stephanie Miller)

My dad and Barry were routed by President Lyndon B. Johnson and his running mate, Senator Hubert Humphrey, in a landslide of historic proportions. The Goldwater-Miller ticket carried just six states and lost by *16 million* votes. I was three years old.

I have reason to think my mother believes that if I had just been a *smidge* more attractive, Dad and Barry might have won the election.

My mother once actually said on national television that I was an unattractive kid. (Later she claimed it was only a joke; now I know where I got *that* excuse from.) "You wouldn't have *recognized* Stephie when she was a child," she told the interviewer. When he asked why, she said, "Oh dear, she was a little *ugly* thing. She's had a lot of work done."

Who needs the National Enquirer when you have a Republican mom? That quote is now burned into my therapist's psyche:

> *"You see, doctor, my mom used to say that I was so ugly, she had to tie a pork chop around my neck to get the dog to play with me…"*

> *"I'm sorry, Stephanie, I'm afraid our time is up for this week."*

> *"I was abandoned by wolves and raised by Republicans!!"*

*"Alright, Stephanie, time to adjust your meds
again...."*

I once showed a friend of mine the official Miller campaign
photo. She said, "Oh my GOD, if he had just held a sack of
potatoes instead of you, he might have at LEAST carried
Idaho."

Here's me, the little spud:

(Photo courtesy of Stephanie Miller)

Of course, I'm lucky my dad ran before campaigns had
all those fancy, high-priced campaign consultants. I'm sure
one of them would have said: "Yikes, Congressman, I'd
just say you lost that youngest one in a nasty wood chipper
accident or something." If they'd had the technology back
then, I would have been Photo Shopped out, or at least
made to look less like a wolf cub and more like Caroline
Kennedy.

As the supposed offspring of a white father and an even
whiter mother (she uses SPF 500 sun block), my parents
went to great lengths to conceal the truth about their furry
little cub. Like President Obama, I was born in 1961. Coin-

cidence? I think *not*. Just like Barack, there's a similar controversy surrounding the facts of my birth. The certificate that my parents hastily manufactured is quite obviously a crude forgery. Thank God there were no psychotically persistent Birthers back in the sixties. Can you imagine Ted Cruz AND the John Birchers?! They would have all been howling wildly at the moon if the GOP had nominated a Vice President who had a secret wolf daughter.

When I was born, my father was not only a congressman, he was also the newly-elected Chairman of the Republican National Committee, which meant he had a national reputation to protect and he knew a wolf cub would not play well with the Republican base. While campaigning for some Republican candidate out west, he got the news from the traveling press corps that his wife, Stephanie, had gone into "labor" (that was just the cover story, since we all know how much Republicans *dislike* labor).

But before the reporters would accept any cigars from my delighted dad, they insisted on knowing the name of the newest Miller.

"Stephanie!" he announced, without hesitation.

This came as something of a shock to my mom, who had already decided that this small feral creature would never bear her name. Surprising though this information was for her, it's hardly the worst piece of news a political spouse has learned from the press. Compared to Hillary Clinton and Huma Abedin, my mother had it easy.

People always ask me what I remember most from my father's 1964 campaign. I give the same answer that Shirley Temple uses to describe her early movies: "It feels like

I'm looking at somebody else up there." To which I can only add, with all the love in my heart, fuck *you*, Shirley Temple. *You* had golden curls and a million dollar smile. I had a unibrow, a natural afro, and gray fangs. (Thanks for the tetracycline, Mom!) Teeth-wise I looked like a cross between Linc from "Mod Squad," and Austin Powers. I can only conjure up vague memories from that time, and I'm sure some of those are really just versions of stories I've heard from my family or things I've read. But the pictures don't lie about what a spooky little spud I was.

(Photo courtesy of Stephanie Miller)

You know that old line about "victory has a thousand fathers, but defeat is an orphan?" The day after the election, my parents dropped me off at the White House with a handwritten note pinned to my little potato-sack dress. It read:

Dear Lady Bird: Congratulations!

After you finish beautifying the highways,
why don't you take a crack at THIS..

There were two important lessons I learned from Dad's 1964 campaign, though they didn't sink in until many years later:

Things always look darkest just before it goes completely black

Somewhere when God shuts a door, he shuts a window too.

And then you're totally fucked.

After November '64, Dad was always clear that while some believe what doesn't kill you only makes you stronger, his experience taught him what doesn't kill you leaves you politically invisible. Hence the title of my sister Libby's book about our father, "Bill Miller: Do You Know Me?" It was based on a highly successful series of American Express commercials from the seventies that featured once prominent public figures—like dad—who had become less well known over time. One thing I learned from my dad early on—if the joke is at your expense, tell it before someone else does!

I also remember Dad saying, "If I'd known we were going to lose by sixteen million votes, I *never* would have worked that hard." Then, as he did after every joke he told, he snorted uncontrollably. He had this volcanic snort, so every time he laughed the silverware flew off the table. It was messy yet heartwarming in a "Father Blows Best" kind of way.

Don't get me wrong, Dad remained an optimist throughout his entire life. And from someone who came across as so mild-mannered, he really was an incredibly funny man. Still, Dad wasn't comfortable letting loose with me until I was much older. It wasn't until I was in college that my father finally shared his more risqué side with me.

I remember that awkward night well when Dad first treated me like a grown-up. My parents took me and my roommate out to dinner. The conversation hit a lull, and my father, out of the blue, said, "Hey, Tina, how do you know a macho woman?"

My roommate, looking puzzled, said, "I don't know. How?"

My father, with a mischievous gleam in his eye: "She has a kick-starter on her vibrator!"

Then he laughed and snorted. The silverware flew. This, of course, elicited my mother's patented response (patent holder: June Cleaver), "Oh, Dear. Oh, Bill."

After the salt and pepper shakers spun to a stop, I stared agape at my parents for about ten seconds. Did my dad, Bill Miller, just tell me and my roommate a *vibrator* joke? *What the...?* I was a 20-year-old sexual unsophisticate and I'd barely even seen a sex toy at that point. I guess by 1981 the '60s free love revolution had finally made it up to Lockport. And...*Mom?* Eww. Is this how they started talking as soon as the baby cub left the den?

I think in many ways I got my ambition from my dad. Even before I had a sense of who he was or what he did, I knew that he was a great man. And I just wanted to do something great like him. I probably related more to him than to my mother in the sense that I looked at my mom and thought, "Hmm…washing pots and pans and raising children. That doesn't seem like the fun job. My dad's job seems much more glamorous. He gets lots of attention and seems very important."

Fame whore, anyone?

Reporters covering the 1964 campaign loved watching my father skewer the notoriously thin-skinned Lyndon Johnson. In fact, Barry Goldwater once joked that the reason he put Dad on the ticket was because of his ability to "drive LBJ nuts."

Since I was an adopted wolf cub, I suppose it's nurture not nature, but I have that same talent—I just use it on random people who *aren't* president. But just for the hell of it, let me give it a political shot and we'll see how I do.

According to Miller family lore, one night, in a more amicable Washington era, LBJ reached across the aisle and asked my mom to dance at some fancy Capital ball. Well, that wasn't the only reach he made. According to my blushing mom, he also played a little grab-ass with her on the dance floor. Not exactly a surprise from the man who named his penis "Jumbo." Of course with those Texas- sized ears of his, he looked a lot more like Dumbo.

See? I just drove LBJ nuts POSTHUMOUSLY. Maybe I *am* Daddy's little girl after all!

My parents were on the campaign trail so much in 1964 that reporters came to our home in Lockport, NY, which is up the transit from Cheektowaga, Lackawanna, and Tonawanda—all Indian names for *"I've got to get the fuck out of here. I'm freezing my tits off!"* A couple of enterprising journalists decided to interview me and my brother, who was five years old. I was barely three. They showed us a picture of our parents. I pointed to it and said, "Oh yes, I remember *them*."

Can you say GAFFE? My father and mother returned home immediately. They stayed just long enough to gag me and my brother—they even taught me how to write my name for the express purpose of making me sign a non-disclosure agreement. Based on that interview alone (my first!), huge swaths of the electorate started peeling away. I bet I did more to convert Republican voters to the other side with that one remark than everything I've said in the last decade on "The Stephanie Miller Show." By age 4, my most persuasive years were already behind me.

Here's Mom and Dad as I remember them best from 1964 (they're on the left, if only compared to the Goldwaters):

(Photo courtesy of Stephanie Miller)

Check out Dad's skinny tie and narrow lapels. I bet I could get some Hollywood hipster to pay me $1,200 for that suit tomorrow. And look at my beautiful mother—wouldn't *you* want to cop a little feel? My parents just thought it was the proper thing to do to leave me and my brother at home. It taught us the traditional American value of self-reliance. And it kept the national press corps from photographing my unibrow.

What they didn't know (at least I like to *think* they didn't know), was that their travels on the campaign trail fit in perfectly with my brother's long-term plan to once again become the youngest Miller child.

Though my parents' political trips surely made it easier for him, my brother's attempts to kill me predated the '64 campaign. Notice I said "attempts"—with an "*s*." I'm sure he would call it euthanasia, but his loving motivation was completely lost on me at the time.

He was the original Death Panel. He once tried to hang me by fashioning a noose, which he hung from the banister. He had a chair all set up.

"Stephie," he beckoned, "step up here and come put your neck in this."

Like a good little sister, I came skipping over and said, "Okay!" What did I know from nooses? I was *three*.

And then he pulled the chair away and I went, "FL-AGARKEN!" which was wolf language for, "GO GET MOM!" But with my neck in the noose, it didn't translate all that well. He heard, "Pull it tighter, Bill!"

If anything can be compared to the look of horror on a mother's face when she sees her youngest child hanging by the neck, it might only be the look on the face of one of Newt Gingrich's wives as he approaches her hospital bed with papers in his hand. All I can remember now is my mother shrieking "Cut her down, Billy! CUT HER DOWN!!"

Which, in my brother's defense, he did. He was the original "compassionate conservative."

Yes, you're saying, "Sibling rivalry, I know about that." But did *your* brother have the foresight to dig a grave for you in the fruit cellar? Mine did. Then he forgot about it. One day my mother went down there to get something for dinner and she fell right into the trench that had been intended for me.

Sure enough, I was the one who got blamed. After all, it was *my* grave.

A firm defender of the 2nd Amendment, my brother would also routinely shoot me with his BB gun. In fairness to him, a one-man militia, I should note that he always gave me a running head start. In fact, the words I remember most from my childhood were "Run, Stephie, run!" I was sort of like a Catholic girl Forrest Gump, but in an incredibly ugly plaid jumper. I do remember in our uneven grade school arms race, that he gave me his hand-me-down bb gun pistol which shot cock-eyed (a harbinger of my later aversion to all things cock-related) to defend myself with, while he had a fancy new state of the art pump action bb rifle. All I remember is hearing the pumping sound before the inevitable "THWACK" sound, as a high-velocity bb arrived in my fleeing back, catapulting me into our well-trimmed Republican hedges.

You can always trust, but verify, that a Republican is going to cheat in an arms race. And possibly illegally arm some right wing rebel friends of theirs, as well.

My brother and I had another game—well, he called it a game, I called it "once again fleeing for my life from my murderous demon-seed sibling." Being an avid football fan, he would yell "Butkus!" which referred to Dick Butkus, the fearsome linebacker for the Chicago Bears in the 60's and early 70's. "Butkus!" would be my cue to run screaming for my life, until my brother caught up with me and held me down like a football in the end zone.

I'll never forget the day he tackled me right into my mother's Ming vase. (I don't know if it actually *was* a Ming vase, but it just sounds like something expensive a '70's mom would have… if you need an '80's reference, it was the glass "egg" from the film *Risky Business*.) If you need a '90's reference, you're on your own, you little whippersnappers… and get off my lawn. Anyway, upon impact, it promptly shattered into a million pieces. In an eerie foreshadowing of how Tea Party Republicans would later blame President Obama for all the crises he was pushed into, Bill immediately pointed to me and said, "Look what you did. Mom's going to *kill* you."

And in a similar foreshadowing of how the press would later handle the Republicans' blatant partisanship and obstructionism, my Mom punished BOTH OF US EQUALLY for "playing in the house." For Bill, it was a never-ending exercise in world domination. *My* side of "playing in the house" was more like my personal version of *Lord of the Flies.*

My brother also had another really fun "game" in which he would hold me down, and drip toothpaste into my face. Although, once again in his defense (liberals always see the other person's point of view), I should say that he sucked it back up into his mouth before it actually *hit* my face, so it really was just an early pre-Gitmo version of waterboarding—but minty, and in very slow motion.

It's sort of ironic that my Dad had been an assistant prosecutor at the Nuremberg Trials, when most of what my brother was doing to me in our own home could technically be categorized as war crimes, and yet it seemed to escape his attention entirely. When I would tell my father what went on in the name of fun while he was at work, he would give one of his signature snorts, pat me and the head and knock back his evening drink. Somehow the Geneva Conventions never came up.

By the way, in case my brother's feeling at *all* litigious, I should add at this point that I also have incredibly fond memories of eating cereal and watching cartoons with him in the big red chair in our den on Saturday mornings. I've been told this is what is known as "Stockholm Syndrome," where one bonds with one's torturer, but when you're sitting together with a bowl of Fruit Loops and sugary milk, anything can be forgiven.

I love you, Bill. (Side note: Bill's a lawyer.)

My mother, God bless her, is still a loyal Republican at the age of 92 and has such a great big heart. I wish I could have half the grace and class she has, but if it hasn't happened by now—and God knows it hasn't—it's not terribly likely that it's ever going to. Of course if I *did* have my mother's elegance and style, I could never pull off the live teabagging demonstration on stage during my Sexy Liberal! comedy show. Did I mention that *The New York Times* called that part of the act "A Chaplinesque example of wordless political theater?" If I didn't mention that, it's because they didn't say it. But as *Hustler* put it in their glowing review, "It's Stephanie Miller's bold artistic attempt to demonstrate the Tea Party's influence on the body politic based on her astonishing personal knowledge of the Kama Sutra."

My family is fair and unbalanced. Do any of you come from a mixed family? If so, you know exactly what I'm talking about here.

How Republican *is* my Mom? Her bird masturbates to Fox News. Seriously. I've seen it ...and I then had to use steel wool to scrape the image from my mind's eye forever. He's a lovebird—in this case, "love" meaning "likes to rub one out to Gretchen Carlson."

His name is "Pretty Boy," he is tethered to a colorful chain, and as soon as Mom turns on the TV, he starts rocking back and forth. When Sean Hannity really gets going, calling the President a *Muslim... Kenyan...Socialist...* the bird starts getting really excited, rocking faster and faster. Feathers flying everywhere, he keeps rocking and rocking, until suddenly there's this loud, disgusting birdgasm sound. Then he just lays down on his little chain, spent. And proud to be an American.

She is *still* in mourning over Glenn Beck leaving Fox. I once said to her, "You know, Mom, I got a lot of death threats from Glenn Beck's crazy fans. "Oh, Stephie"—she really has said this—"I don't appreciate you calling Glenn Beck's fans *crazy*."

Um…maybe she missed the part about…oh, never mind.

I think if one of his fans only winged me with a wild shot or the Book of Mormon hurled at my head—nothing fatal, just a little blood loss—she'd still attend *his* press conference.

"Oh, Glenn, Stephie's gotten so *radical*. Don't blame yourself. I'm sure it was something she said."

My Mom actually wrote a fan letter to George W. Bush about how he was THE GREATEST PRESIDENT WE'VE EVER HAD. She had me sit in front of her while she read the whole thing out loud. Slowly. She is part of that great generation that still considers proper enunciation a patriotic virtue. Of course, since Mom doesn't have a computer because, like the cell phone, it is a liberal tool of Satan, it was hand-written, and did I mention VERY long? *Roget's Thesaurus* doesn't have as many synonyms for "manly" as she had in the first paragraph.

Me: "Uh huh. Uh huh. Right. Uh huh. Okay, Mom , well that was nice. I think he's a *war criminal*."

You know what she said? Of course you do.

Mom: "Oh, Stephie, you've gotten so *radical*."

My mom is the kind of person—don't get me wrong, I love her so dearly—but my mom is the kind of Republican who believes that no Republican is ever bad. So if George W. Bush had fucked a sheep on the White House lawn and then set it on fire, my mother would have said, "Oh, Stephie, the President's doing the best he can. The sheep looked lonely. And cold. Why do you hate America so much?"

I've told my mother how much I admire her and Dad for the way they protected us from being exploited for cheap political purposes. My mother and father came from an era when vice presidential candidates had the innate decency *not* to use their small children as campaign props.

Unlike my father's era, we now live in a time when "family values" is just a slogan used to win votes. And, yes, I'm talkin' about *you*, Caribou Barbie. (By the way, and just for the record, it should be noted that *I* was the very first person to tag Sarah Palin with that nickname. Then *everybody* started using it. Damn! Why didn't I trademark it when she was still relevant?)

When that pouty-mouthed Eddie Munster, Paul Ryan, was picked as Mitt Romney's running mate, I was touched when Rachel Maddow used the occasion to say some really nice things about my dad:

> *"One more thing about Bill Miller, Barry Goldwater's pick for vice president in 1964. Yes, Bill Miller and Barry Goldwater got beaten really, really badly in 1964, the Republicans' worst presidential showing ever. Johnson and the Democrats beat them by over twenty points. And, yes, Bill Miller was lost enough to obscurity that a decade later he did one of those American Express "Do You Know Me?" ads where the whole idea of the*

ad was, of course, that you didn't know who this person was.

But there's one thing about Bill Miller besides being Barry Goldwater's vice president and being in that American Express ad and his previous career in politics and the military, there's one thing that really does survive the years about Bill Miller, for which he still to this day is totally, justifiably famous in a very positive way. And that is that he is Stephanie Miller's dad! Stephanie Miller, the high priestess of excellent liberal talk radio. Her dad was Bill Miller, Barry Goldwater's vice president. And it is conclusive evidence of a life well lived that she is his daughter."

What a kind thing—even though I consider myself to be the least of my father's accomplishments. She also called him a *true* conservative, in contrast to today's party of reflexive reactionary rigidity, and graciously acknowledged my father's long career in public life. And she even mentioned me. It helps that Rachel's own dad, Bob, listens to my show daily, and emails me every so often. Rachel actually once told me: "My Dad calls me EVERY DAY to tell me what you said on your show that morning." I can only imagine what's in *her* thought bubble: "Ok, Dad, I'm a Rhodes scholar with an incredibly successful television career...*she* tells fart jokes. But thanks for the news update!" I actually once spilled wine on every member of the Maddow family simultaneously, including Rachel and her lovely mother, Elaine, at an event in Seattle in the early days of progressive radio, in some sort of really awkward liberal baptism. Rachel was the moderator of that event, and I recall as she took audience questions on cue cards, she remarked that the most frequent question asked was: "Will Stephanie sign my ass after this event?" It's a wonder anyone in that family still associates with me in ANY way, though I like to think that it's because they all credit that moment with being the final catalyst that clearly spurred her to such great heights...and as far away from ME as possible.

Sadly, my own dad passed just after I graduated college, as I'll get to later. I obviously learned neither oratory nor political strategy from him, just as he had no talent for imitating Katharine Hepburn. He wasn't the kind of person for whom politics was just self-promotion and theatrics. I know that my father didn't fully understand my desire to become a performer, but he always supported and loved me unconditionally.

My mother, thank God, is still with us. I've been fortunate to have her love and support for my entire adult life. Some kids don't get to keep publicly embarrassing their parents with dick jokes past puberty. I'm one lucky cub.

Dad's service to our country and his courage still inspire me every day. It's been more than thirty years since we lost him, but I will miss him always. As I said, I wanted to be great like him. That sure didn't happen, but like him I can tell a great vibrator joke. And I am incredibly proud to be his daughter.

I'M STILL BIG, IT'S THE RADIO THAT GOT SMALL

Every woman broadcaster remembers her first microphone. It's like her first penis. The shape is essentially the same and men are disproportionately defensive about both. You have to wonder about the hypocrisy of middle-aged right-wing radio guys screaming about the gays when they've decided to earn their living mouthing off into a phallus for three hours a day. In this male-dominated business, men will protect a microphone like it's their *actual* dick. Or, like Rush Limbaugh (who hasn't actually *seen* his junk since Dan Quayle was vice president), they have their microphones gold-plated. I guess nobody told El Rushbo that gold is one of the softest metals around.

No matter how much women try to make men believe size is no big deal, size really DOES matter. Especially with microphones. You can fit your mouth around a tiny one, but it usually has a very small signal. Remember the movie "Alien?" In a 10,000 watt station, nobody can hear you scream. That's the fate of most liberal talk show hosts: the station's at the low end of the dial, so even if you're next to the fucking tower, it sounds like a broadcast from the '30s that bounced back to Earth off a piece of space debris.

I was 21 when I got my first job in radio. It was 1983 and I'd just graduated from USC with a drama degree, which of course would guarantee me a job in virtually ANY 7-Eleven in the world.

Turns out that my prestigious academic credential prepared me far less for a professional career in the theater than it did for all the drama life had in store for me (although my minor in Histrionics has turned out to be a HUGE help to me throughout my broadcasting career).

Here's the truth, parents. A degree in drama will give your child invaluable training for the Slurpee/barista job they will get immediately after graduation (while still living in their old room in your house). There's nothing like four years of Ibsen and Chekhov to prepare them for "Was that a double decaf espresso chai latte, you fucking entitled asshole?"

It's like I tell college students at speeches when they come up to me afterwards, all earnest and doe-eyed, and ask me, "How can we become a star like *you*, Stephanie?"

"Well you can't because there's no more *room* left in radio, but good luck." Then I turn dramatically on my stilettos and stride quickly away. Suddenly I stop and pivot back to face them. Mama knows exactly how to take a crushed dream and grind it even farther into the ground. "Perfect your craft, kids," I say compassionately, taking a deep drag from a cigarette (and then hocking up a huge loogie because I don't smoke). "And if that doesn't work, get really good at oral sex."

After graduating USC, I quickly landed a highly promising position in LA selling customized pens over the phone. "How do you sell pens over the phone?" you might ask. The short answer: You don't.

Turns out I got into this cutting-edge profession just as the axe was coming down on the customized pen industry. There had been what business analysts called an unprecedented technological disruption. I called them "FUCKING JOB KILLING ROBOT WRITERS!" Word processors were now the rage in offices everywhere. Fear filled the air. All over town people were saying, "Pens are OVER." This was the same unfortunate timing that would come to characterize my entire future career—but I didn't know it then. The Universe has never been my friend (although we still exchange holiday cards). I had planned to stay in La La Land until I'd either taken over for Johnny Carson ("Heeeere's Stephie!") or just been given my own network. My timeline of three months to be crowned the Queen of Television was, in retrospect, a tad unrealistic.

First of all, I didn't even have an agent and, as it turned out, Johnny wasn't going anywhere for another decade. But I was undeterred. Reality didn't intrude on my dreams of stardom.

Until it did.

I'd only been out of college for a few weeks when my mother called to give me frightening and completely unexpected news about my father. She said, "You need to come home right now, Stephanie. Dad is in the hospital." I was numb. I'd just seen my father at graduation, and he'd seemed completely fine. My mom had mentioned something to me, almost in passing. She'd said, "Oh you know, Daddy needs to have a test. He's lost vision a couple times in his right eye, which can be a warning sign for a stroke, but we're sure it's nothing to worry about. He's just going in for a test; it's no big deal, so we decided to wait until after your graduation."

I put down the phone and sat there on my bed, dazed. Just weeks before my dad and I were sitting together on that same bed and he'd said, "You know, Stephie, I'm so proud of you, and as long as I'm alive I'll take care of you, don't worry," in that incredibly kind, loving, protective, fatherly way of his.

I packed my bags, tossed a handful of personalized pens into the wastebasket (the customers at Cheese Please Pizza would have to order their slices without my help) and headed directly to the airport.

By the time I landed in Buffalo, it was clear that my father wasn't doing well. At only 69 years old, he'd gone in for what should have been a routine angiogram. But apparently the procedure had shaken loose some particles of plaque, which turned into life-threatening blood clots, that actually caused a stroke and then, finally, a coma. I remember before the coma, he asked me how long I would be home. I said: "Until you get better, Daddy!" Two weeks later he was gone. It was June 24, 1983. I remember talking to him some while he was in the coma, but I didn't think he could hear me, so I mostly just held his hand and cried. Years later, I read an article on how doctors now thought that people in comas CAN actually hear and are aware much more than was previously thought. To this day, I regret the things I didn't say to my Dad the very last time I had a chance. I know I would have thanked him for all he sacrificed to allow me the life I had, how proud I was of him and the wonderful legacy he left our family. It's remarkable how powerful regret is and how it drives some of our greatest music. I had the opportunity to tell James Taylor, when I was fortunate enough to interview him on my radio show, that the very first song I heard when I got in my car right after my Dad died, was "Fire and Rain."

The moment and the memory are still seared in my heart every time I hear those lyrics: *But I always thought I'd see you again…*

Everybody was numb. My Mom told me that the evening before he went into the hospital for the test, Dad and Mom had danced together late into the night at a wedding reception. Speaking of music and memories, Luther Vandross' "Dance With My Father Again" is another song I have never gotten through once without dissolving in tears. Trust me, break-up songs after a breakup are NOTHING compared to songs that remind you of losing one of the only two people in the world that you can never ever replace in your life, your parents. Dancing with my mother, that's the image of my father that I will always carry in my heart. A man who enjoyed life fully and always knew how to have fun—and to share that joy of life with everyone around him. My last Christmas with my Dad, just six months earlier, summed up exactly who he was as a man, and as a father. When I showed him a videotape of a comedy show I had written and starred in at USC, he said: "YOU did all that? By God, Stephie, I don't know much about show business, but I think you're gonna make it! I said "Oh, Daddy, I just want to be half as great as you are someday." And he said: "Oh, honey, I think you're going to be far greater than I ever was." That says everything you need to know about what a truly kind, humble, loving man he was. As it turns out, he was incredibly WRONG…but still really kind, right? And funny. My other memory of our last Christmas was when my Mom sat down and started playing the piano, he turned to me and said: "Great, just what we need…another Polack on the piano." I'm pretty sure she burned his Pierogies that Christmas on purpose, but who can say?

As a grieving Barry Goldwater said at the funeral of his friend and running mate, "Yes, he served well. He served with love and devotion to his wonderful family. He served with love and devotion to his country…Because of these things, and because of the way he was, and to me is, he made every one of us better, and he made this country a better place to live." He also said, "He was a man other men liked to be with." Which, of course, some comedy shows back then turned into a gay joke which I cannot tell you, on how many levels, I did not appreciate at the time.

Daddy was buried with full military honors at Arlington National Cemetery, right near JFK's grave with the famous "eternal flame." Interesting historically, since President Kennedy's sad fate led directly to the make-up of the 1964 election, which led, of course, to my Dad's place in political history. I always found it fascinating to learn that JFK and Goldwater actually liked each other very much, and were really looking forward to debating and running against each other in 1964. And my Dad who, as Chairman of the Republican National Committee, was in St. Louis at a Republican gathering the day President Kennedy was shot, said eloquently and simply to the St. Louis newspaper, "We are Americans first and Republicans second." It was a very different time in our partisan history, to say the least.

After the ceremony, all of us returned to Lockport. As much as I missed my father, my mother missed him more than I can imagine. They had a 40-year conversation that ended abruptly. Right then I felt like my mother needed me, since no one else in the family lived in Buffalo at the time, so it wasn't even a question of what I would do. Stardom (or whatever was waiting for me in my post-personalized-pen career) would have to wait. I moved back to Lockport or, as I like to call it, the "Lesser Buffalo Area." Actually, I had already taken a summer job as a guide at "Artpark," a performing arts park in Niagara County, in anticipation of being there for my Mom and Dad during what I had hoped would be my Dad's recovery. I also met my very first girl-friend, Molly, there (or llllesbian lllllover as Tom Brokaw would say... badllllly).

Now Buffalo and Hollywood aren't that different, except for EVERYTHING. Hollywood has the Sunset Strip, but in Buffalo, *every* street is a Boulevard of Broken Dreams. In LA I had been in a sketch comedy group, I performed in theater, certain I was going to become the next Carol Burnett. After a time, with my mom seeming much better (though I'm sure she wasn't), she and I both agreed I should move back to Los Angeles and resume my non-existent show business career. This, of course, ended up consisting of me answering the phones at "The Laugh Factory," and changing the names of the famous comedians on the mar-quee with a giant pole. This may have led to my later fear and aversion to poles of any kind, giant or not. I remember cursing Paul Rodriguez once, as one of his many vowels, or maybe it was a consonant, hit me in the face. "Damn you, Paul Rodriguez, one day MY NAME will be up there!" And, cue magic wand sound effect...one day it was. I also cocktail waitressed at the Laugh Factory to buttress my al-ready exorbitant phone answering/pole handling income, and all I remember is that the sub-contractor at the time didn't have enough glasses to serve people and constantly beseeched me in some weird accent : "The glaaaaases, dar-ling, get the glasssses, we don't have enough clean glassssses to keep serving the peoples." She was like some mutant love child of Arianna Huffington and Imelda Marcos. Ah, this grand business we call SHOW.

After several months, I got the bright idea that I should move back to Buffalo, and debut my own one woman com-edy show, like Whoopi Goldberg had just done on Broad-way to great acclaim.

I oddly named it "Stephanie Miller: Out of the Comedy Closet," for a woman that was CLEARLY not out of the gay closet yet. Perhaps I was irony deficient. Anyway, it de-buted to "meh-ves," a combination of raves, and "meh," as my Jewish comedy friends would say. And also, did I men-tion it was in FUCKING BUFFALO???? What the FUCK was I thinking? My big sister, who was a news reporter at the local Buffalo TV station then, and who had become my de facto PR agent/Mafioso enforcer, strong-armed her friend, Sally, who was the host of the local P.M. Magazine show, to go do a story on my pre-Broadway triumph. She did, and Sally later became my lovah (it turns out Buffalo was hotter than I thought). Mama was ready for her close-up…in sooooo many ways. Grrrr.

After my theatrical triumph, I soared to a MUCH higher level than I had ever reached in Los Angeles…in Buffalo I answered the phone at Yuk Yuks, the local comedy club and the center of the white-cold Upstate comedy scene. Also, did I mention I was back in FUCKING BUFFALO??? I was living in a $125 a month apartment over a pizza parlor across the street from the club. Though still terrified, I was also doing occasional stand-up routines. More accurately, they should have been called "crouch down" routines, as that was the usual position I found myself in to avoid being hit by flying objects. My new life may have represented a step up from selling pens in Los Angeles, but it was a whole elevator shaft down because...well, it was *Buffalo*.

For a brief time, I thought seriously about joining the Peace Corps, not out of a principled commitment to improving the world, but because, like most liberal arts majors, I was woefully unprepared for what it took to begin a real adult life. Building shelters and educating the poor seemed like just the thing to occupy my time while I cooked up a scheme to break into showbiz. I watched a *lot* of "I Love Lucy" growing up. When I told my brother Bill my plan, he said, "Whatever, Drama Degree, what are you going to do—teach them how to *act* like they're not hungry?"

Shortly after, when my not-yet-but-soon-to-be lovah, Sally, was co-hosting a morning drive radio show, she encouraged me to come into the studio and do my uncanny impressions of Linda Blair and Katharine Hepburn live on the air. The other host was Sandy Beach *("Sandy Beach in the morning, everybody! WNYS Hot 104 in Buffalo, NY, everybody!")*, and he had me do everything from the weather to traffic reports. Sandy was the only beach most Buffalonians knew. Hot 104 turned out to be great place to get my start. *That* was where I blew my first microphone.

I still hear from people who remember my *Exorcist*-inspired weather forecasts *("Your mother sucks popsicles on Lake Erie, it's gonna be hot as HELL in Buffalo tomorrow!")*. And I KILLED every time I did my shaky-voiced Kate Hepburn in a traffic *"coptah"*: *"I'd leave early, if you're going up the Transit this morning, you old poops! It's gonna be a looooong ride, riide, riiide. There's trouble on the Scajaquada Express-*

way. Listen to me, there's a greeeeaaaat big COW chip on the shouldah!"

When you're 21, your employers treat you like you ought to be grateful just to have a job and bring them coffee. Since I only had a tiny microphone to fellate, the program director at WNYS expected me to be a happy little girl who didn't need to get paid. At one point, they *did* offer me a bicycle (as if my job were a paper route), but I never even got a three-wheeler.

Radio was a complete accident for me, but I didn't care. I figured it was helping me hone the necessary skills that would eventually get me the job I *really* wanted, becoming the next Carol Burnett. And if that didn't work out, move over Traci Lords—there's not enough room in this bed for both of us!

My astonishing talent soon earned me my own show— "Miller in the Morning"—on WLVL, an oldies station in my hometown of Lockport, NY. The station was so old ("How old *was* it?") that I had to run back and forth changing the reel-to-reel tapes myself or there'd be dead air. It was a total time warp: the Beach Boys and The Supremes and The Four Seasons all day—the soundtrack from the season of dad's 1964 campaign had come back to life for me as an adult. It was trial by fire for the new kid, but they let me do my thing. One morning I did a tour-de-force opening monologue of all two of my greatest hits—Katharine Hepburn *and* Linda Blair. While I was still in mid-monologue, I was certain the Smithsonian was already calling for the tape. There was only one problem—I'd forgotten to turn on my tiny microphone. Oddly, not a *single* person called to inquire about the silence. Not even the program director who, as luck would have it, never woke up before noon. More people would have heard me if I'd just thrown open a window and shouted the traffic reports down to the street.

Despite what should have been a career-ending gaffe, I was soon called up to the big leagues—Rochester—where I joined "Brother Wease's Morning Circus," the top-rated show in the market. Don't laugh—I went from a town of 25,000 to a city of almost 250,000 people. Granted it was only an hour away, and the most glamorous place in Rochester was the Kodak plant, but for an Armenian wolf cub from Lockport, this was my big break.

Alan Levin—aka Brother Wease—is one of the kindest people I've ever worked with. He had been searching for a sidekick, and hearing my classy shtick on one of the days I remembered to turn the mic on, he thought his radio dreams had come true. He quickly made me feel like family, even christening me "Sister Sleaze." We became "Brother Wease and Sister Sleaze." It was rock 'n' roll radio, so I was at least occasionally in the current musical decade, mixing some Joan Jett and Pat Benatar in with the already classic Led Zeppelin and Rolling Stones hits. The highlight was broadcasting naked in a barrel with Brother Wease in a storefront window to promote…oh, who can remember? Paint? Leaf blowers? It was one of those wacky eighties DJ stunts that involved nudity and gave us another two weeks of mindless morning chatter. But I had become part of a local institution and, at this point, I was now a radio *professional*. My older sister Libby, while vacationing on a beach in New Zealand, somehow got into a conversation with a fellow tourist about her baby sibling, the DJ. "Oh my

God," said the astonished woman, "You're Sister Sleeze's *sister*?!" Libby was mortified. My embarrassing reputation had gone global. Brother Wease brought me a whole new level of radio fame (not to be confused with actual fame). To this day people from Rochester call into my show and say "Hey, Sleaze!" Well, at least they *pretend* to be from Rochester.

Wease and I did lots of gags and a good deal of celebrity baiting. It was great training for what I do now. In fact, I still tell the same timely "Karate Kid" and "Footloose" jokes today. But that's largely because when you get to be my age, it's as if you desperately want the world to become an oldies station. Believe me, it's a painful and pitiful experience for me to make an on-air reference to Meathead from "All in the Family" and get only blank stares back from the interns. Fuck you, jail bait! Read a book with more than 140 characters.

But, as old people do to the perpetual annoyance of the young, I digress. Back in those early days, I was just a kid myself—a morning zoo girl with a port-a-potty mouth. My mother always said, "Oh, Stephie, why do you have *use* such language?" To which I could only reply, "What the fuck, mom! It's *comedy*, for Christ's sake."

Even now, this remains an ongoing conversation with my mother. "Why can't you be more like that nice Rita Rudner?" Mom invariably asks. "She never works blue and *she* wears a dress." That bitch Rita taunts me about it whenever I see her at a strip club.

I'm certainly no George Carlin. When I say shit, piss, fuck, cunt, cocksucker, motherfucker or tits, it's never on-the-air. Those words only come out of my mouth when I'm standing behind someone in the supermarket checkout line who's buying groceries with a bag of pennies (counted out one at a time) or when I'm being over-groped at an airport by a pervy TSA agent with saliva drooling down his chin.

When I'm on the air now, I rely on my brilliant producer, "Lightning" Chris Lavoie, to keep me from fuck...er, *screwing* up. He has what we broadcast professionals un-ironically call a "dump" button. There's a mandatory seven-second delay on any live broadcast. This means Chris can catch any verboten word within seven seconds of my saying it and my listeners only hear silence. I also self-police with my personal box (SOUND EFFECTS BOX, you dirty little people), a device that allows me to insert bleeps in place of obscenities. It's like a trans-vaginal sound effects machine. Seems foolproof, right? But nothing is foolproof if you're a big enough fool.

I always said that radio was a complete accident until I started to actually make a lot of money and it wasn't really an accident anymore.

But every accident that you can walk away from—or make money from—has a guardian angel. Mine was a kind, brilliant woman named Lily Tomlin who didn't know me from Eve. She was doing a national stage tour of "Search for Signs of Intelligent Life in the Universe." I tried to get a personal interview with her on my radio show and couldn't because, well...she was LILY FUCKING TOMLIN, and I was a dweeb radio DJ in Chicago. She held a press conference where she took questions about the show. After attending it, I went back to my station and edited all her answers to make it sound like I was the only one asking all the questions, and she had incredibly hilarious answers to every one. I sent it to her PR person, who sent it to Lily... who loved it!! Nothin' but net, as my basketball bull dyke friends would say. *Swish.* Before she left Chicago, she called into my radio show as Ernestine, which was surreal. The best part for me was that her PR person called after the interview to say, "Lily wanted to know if you thought it was ok, if she was funny." The longest pause in telephone history. Lily Tomlin wanted to know if, *I*, Stephanie Miller, thought *she* was funny? Umm...yes, she's Lily Tomlin, for the love of Jesus-H.-fucking-comedy-legend-on-a-popsicle-stick! That gave me a window into how real Lily Tomlin is, something I would later learn is all too rare in this business.

A few years later, when I finally met her in person on my morning drive show on Hot 97 in New York City (Mama had hit the big time), my eyes were wide as saucers, but it was radio, so nobody could see. It was Lily Tomlin, just sitting there talking to *me*. I would have pinched myself, but I bruise easily. Somehow, despite my fan-girl babbling, I made a favorable impression on her. I think her headphones weren't turned on, so she only saw my lips moving—mime radio. Mama was livin' the dream in 1989!

(Quick sidebar on the road to Hollywood history. Around this time I co-hosted "Short Attention Span Theater" a few times on Comedy Central with a guy named Jon Stewart, who I knew had absolutely no future in broadcasting. I asked my friends, "Why are they pairing me with this little loser, Jon Stewart? He's obviously not going anywhere from this.")

When it comes to talent, Mama's intuition is like a broken Geiger counter: I'm drawn to inert metals like lead. Point me at Corey Feldman and my clicker goes mad. Anyone with real potential is completely impossible for me to recognize. Now Mama only sticks to stock predictions, like her famous "Buy Enron!" moment that is still talked about on Wall Street. And in the Justice Department.

Anyway, as is the case in radio, your contract is always just about to be up for renewal and while mine was under review at Hot 97 (we were getting good ratings, so I wasn't worried), I got offered a sitcom deal with Warner Bros for one of the many "You're-going-to-be-the-next-Mary Tyler Moore"-projects, as they promised every young female actress in the early 90's. Each prospective Spunkette was even given a choice of hats to throw in the air for their promotional tape. For some reason, I chose a baseball hat made of concrete.

Here's where the Angel Lily comes in. Lily Tomlin got me my first agent at ICM. I didn't even *ask* her for help. During the commercial break in our interview, I mentioned, almost in passing, "I have this sitcom offer and I don't have an agent." She called her reps at ICM and got me in the door because she's unlike almost any other comedian I've ever met—a genuinely caring, unselfish person who enjoys helping other people succeed. I heard the words that a no-name loser dweeb never expects to hear: "Lily Tomlin called us about you."

Obviously, she was never issued the Comic's Handbook, secretly published in the Catskills in 1926. I'm told Milton Berle stole it from Henny Youngman and never gave him credit. Which, coincidentally, is the First Rule of the Handbook: Screw Thy Competition Before He Can Screw

You. Comics are not nice people. Except Lily and Jane Wagner. And of course anyone else who may someday have me on their show as a guest, or give me a job, or send me a holiday card, or not steal my dogs. Love ya, Jon Stewart! Remember me?

I hadn't decided to roll the dice on the sitcom, but the Universe which, with all respect to Lily and Jane, has never shown me any signs of intelligence, decided to make the choice for me. The New York station had become more, as they say in radio business-speak, "urban." Or, in the words of my equally caucasian co-host when we interviewed the wildly popular African-American teenage duo KRISS KROSS: "I feel like an old, white dinosaur." That's when I knew it was time for me to try television. But to this day, I'm not sure if I jumped or was pushed out of Hot 97.

So I loaded up with #45 sunscreen, hopped on the big bird to Los Angeles and prepared to knock 'em dead. "You're Gonna Make It After All!"

Not so much. The moment I moved to Los Angeles, everyone from Warner Brothers got fired, including all the people who had made my sitcom deal. As I insisted to the security guard at the studio gate, where my name *wasn't* on the list, "But you don't UNDERSTAND. I just gave up my radio show and moved to Los Angeles. I'm a sitcom star now! Check that mother-fucking list again or I'll have your badge! Do you know who I am?" They said "no." When they finally forced me to turn my car around, I could hear the man who'd just killed my career say to one of the other guards, "Poor girl. She's seen *Sunset Boulevard* too many times."

Yet somehow, I still wasn't worried. As the boys in "Spinal Tap" (my friend Rob Reiner's brilliant mockumentary of a rock and roll band that keeps finding new ways to fail) famously put it, "There's a fine line between stupid and clever." I kept acting as if this was all part of my larger plan. The phrase you're looking for is delusions of grandeur, because on a completely objective basis, I was totally out of work.

I rented a house in Nichols Canyon in the Hollywood Hills, which I shared with a woman named Patty, a fitness trainer who traveled often. It wasn't really a relationship, but I wasn't completely alone either (By the way have you picked up at this point that I'm a giant carpet muncher? You can read all the juicy details in my next book, "Who Let the Dykes Out?!").

Soon after, I got a lucky break. Remember Yuk Yuk's, the Buffalo comedy club where I answered phones? The manager there knew the program director of KFI in Los Angeles, called him about me, the star-in-waiting, and I got a weekend talk show there.

KFI is one of the biggest radio stations in the country (its signal is so powerful you can hear it on the moon—we used to get a lot of calls from the Sea of Tranquility). Understand, I'd never actually done talk radio. At this point, I'd had a radio career in either Top 40 morning drive or Classic Rock morning drive, but never in the talk format. However, out of desperation, and in a perfect mix of stupid AND clever, I said, "Why, I'd love to do a talk radio show on the weekend."

That first day, I was terrified. I have to talk for HOW long? My first segment was the longest uninterrupted period of time I'd ever been live on-air because I was used to Top 40 radio, where the rule is "Be funny, do it in 18 seconds, and hit the post before the song starts. It was always "More music in the morning, everybody!" Also, I was used to having a co-host.

All of a sudden it was ten to twelve minutes of just uninterrupted ME. So I began with "Blah, Blah, Blah, Blah" and "Oh, by the way, Blah!" Back to me again? "Of course," I added, "You can't forget Blah, Blah AND Blah." Oh, shit. Only two minutes in?!! "Blabbetty, Blabbetty, Blah!" Though naturally talkative, I wasn't immediately used to being chatty in that format.

Somehow I got through it. Part of it was discovering that you could talk to yourself for long stretches at a time and not be a psychotic person. Or, in the case of some of our wildly popular conservative talk hosts, their natural psychosis is an asset. Certainly they win handily in that demo. Let's just say that most of them would be talking to themselves in a little padded room anyway, so why NOT get paid for it? Actually, Dr. Laura was sort of my mentor at that point, clearly not having realized that I was "a biological mistake," as she called gay people back then.

Despite my incompetence, the show was spectacularly successful, and the ratings were terrific, So much so, that KFI gave me a full-time, five day a week show. I replaced former Los Angeles police chief, Daryl Gates. I remember the program director telling me he was scared to fire Daryl Gates because he was a very intimidating man and that's why he took him to lunch in a very public place to do it. Chief Gates passed away a few years ago, so I finally feel safe taking the phony registration number off my license plates.

It was 1994, and I quickly shot to the top of the ratings on the strength of the number one talk topic in America: Orenthal James Simpson. O.J. was the only subject that could make all the phone lines light up in 30 seconds. His name quickly replaced "blah" in my on-air vocabulary :" OJ, OJ, MURDERER, OJ, KATO, KATO, OJ, BLAN-CO BRONCO!"

What was it that Hunter S. Thompson said? "When the going gets weird, the weird turn pro." The truly *weird* thing about my show on KFI was that it landed me another TV offer. I was only on for a month, and still only on weekends, when an executive at Disney, who was a big fan, offered me a new television development deal.

The Disney offer was for a syndicated late night television show in the same spot originally occupied by Arsenio Hall. Now Arsenio was a pal of mine and I liked him, he even invited me to hang out from time to time, we didn't "Hollywood date" like Barry "Greg Brady" Williams and I who, thanks to our publicists, involved cameras, red carpets, air kisses, and no sex. In real life, as we now all know, Florence "Mrs. Brady" Henderson got more meat from Barry than I did, or than even Alice got from Sam the butcher.

In the spring of 1994, Arsenio quit his show. After he left, Viacom syndicated "The Jon Stewart Show" (remember him?) in Arsenio's old slot. Unfortunately for my former "Short Attention Span Theater" co-host, many of Arsenio's former affiliates had moved his fading show to 2:00 AM, never a good time to get people giggling. Even if they are awake, they're usually giggling on their own, and do not require the help of a talk show host. Poor Jon inherited those deadly time slots and got...crickets. His show was canceled in June 1995.

Enter Mama! The Disney people promised me the moon, the stars, and Cinderella's carriage: an earlier time slot. There was only one condition: I would have to give up my radio show. Even though my patron saint at Disney was the fan who loved me on radio, HER legal department threatened action against KFI if I continued doing the radio show after my late night show debuted. More stupid than clever, I argued that the extra exposure would be good for the television show. The Mousekattorneys begged to differ. Rat fangs bared, they snarled that I could not be in "first position" with two separate entertainment companies and I would have to choose. They had me in "first position" and several others, all of them painful. I was being fucked, and not in a good way, and without lube, AND without even being told I was pretty first.

Employing my unique super-power for making smart career moves, I chose television. "The Stephanie Miller," which premiered to great fanfare in September 1995, lasted a lucky 13 weeks. Mama would soon perfect her God-Given talent to sink individual TV shows into an almost uncanny ability to destroy entire networks. (More on THAT in my next book: "How I Killed Oprah.")

"Hi ho, hi ho, it's back to radio we go!" KFI offered to put me back on only in Los Angeles, but now that Mama had tasted a national audience, however briefly, she needed it back. *Bad.* Trust me, national syndication is like crack. Once you've had it you're hooked for life. So I accepted an offer from KABC that syndicated me in 13 other markets. Hello again, Cleveland!

In 1998 the number one talk subject went abruptly from Broncos to blow jobs—specifically, Bill Clinton's. It was a comedian's dream come true. The top story for two years was essentially a dick joke. Even Dan Rather had to say "penis" every night on the air. I was in heaven.

I'd never talked much about politics on the air. People knew who my father was and they knew I was the liberal (if still closeted) fruit that fell from a conservative tree. Until I got to KABC, I paid more attention to The Supremes than the Supreme Court. But somehow, at that point, I was ready. That was one closet door I was prepared to open.

Mama's personal political epiphany had happened a few years earlier. Maybe it was because I grew up in a political household and wanted to move in the other direction, or maybe it was because by the time I was old enough to be aware of who my dad was, he'd already left politics behind, but I really didn't think about how politics affected our lives until August 1992. I was just a comedian—that's all I ever wanted to be. Unless you considered "Exorcist" weather reports anti-Catholic, it was just another 18-second joke.

But then crazy Pat Buchanan's face filled my television set and it all changed. The Democratic National Convention in New York City had wound up just a few weeks before. Clinton was characteristically magnetic and amazing and I remember the feeling, watching Bill dance with Hillary and Al dance with Tipper (ah, how innocent we were), that after 12 years of Reaganism (including Poppy Bush), "Now it's *our* turn."

Buchanan was always a pit bull, since his days as Nixon's speechwriter. Predictably, he used this high-profile moment to try and turn the clock backwards rather than "THINKING ABOUT TOMORROW" as Bill and the Democrats had left us all singing after their convention. But no one quite expected the bile that spewed from Buchanan's mouth. He was Fox News before there *was* a Fox News.

"Like many of you last month," he began, "I watched that giant masquerade ball at Madison Square Garden—where 20,000 radicals and liberals came dressed up as moderates and centrists—in the greatest single exhibition of cross-dressing in American political history."

Crossdressing? I didn't know where this was going, but it couldn't be good.

"The malcontents of Madison Square Garden notwith-standing," he bleated, "the 1980s were not terrible years. They were great years. You know it. I know it. And the only people who don't know it are the carping critics who sat on the sidelines of history, jeering at one of the great statesmen of modern times."

Was he kidding? The savings and loan crisis, Iran-Contra, and, worst of all, the complete indifference to the AIDS epidemic. That's when my switch was flipped.

"We stand against the amoral idea that gay and lesbian couples should have the same standing in law as married men and women," he thundered.

This was his famous "Culture War" speech, and I know I wasn't the only one who was politicized that day. But it was more than just the liberal bashing that did it. I may not have been out publicly, but these remarks cut very deep with me.

While he wasn't my first boyfriend, Tim Nelson was the first person I ever fell in love with. Well, as much as I could tell what love even was at the time. We were in high school, and it was hard to compare it to anything, but Tim and I *called* ourselves in love. He thought I was cute and funny, he was a lifeguard: the perfect couple. He was the person I practiced being in love with and he with me. We hung out, we made out, and we made each other laugh.

Like so many high school romances we pledged that we'd love each other forever. We had the obligatory emotional goodbye when we went off to college. "You'll always be the love of my life!" "We'll always stay together!" We just *got* each other, and, as you do then, I thought we'd be together and happy the rest of our lives. And it's true, we never lost touch.

We were both back home in Lockport for Christmas sometime in the late '80s when a mutual friend told me Tim was sick. "What do you mean 'sick'?" That's when Tim and I went out for drinks and he told me, "I'm gay and I have AIDS." It was back in those "great" Reagan years, before there was an HIV cocktail, before the government even acknowledged there was crisis. He was one of those poor souls who had to come out to his family *and* tell them he had AIDS at the same time. One person close to him responded: "AIDS? What are you—a faggot?"

It was some years later, before Tim died, that we admitted to each other that, yeah, we both suspected *something* was up with the other one. We laughed so hard at the thought of us back then. I finally asked, "So, when were you with your first guy?"

"The summer after high school," he said.

"Oh, ok... Wait a minute... WHAT THE FUCK!? You mean right after we pledged to be the love of each other's lives? Where did you *meet* him?"

"At the beach."

My lifeguard boyfriend's first gay experience was with a guy he met at the beach. Cue the queerest version of "Summer Lovin'" EVER.

Tim died right before my late night show debuted. He had the advertisement for the show with my picture on the bulletin board in his hospital room and he made a point of telling all the nurses, "That's my girlfriend."

Buchanan's speech changed everything for me. That reactionary bully was saying that people like Tim and I didn't deserve the same rights as a dirtbag like him? At that moment I stepped out and proud as a liberal.

After Monica Lewinsky replaced OJ on the tip of everyone's tongue, I found myself getting pissed, but not at Bill Clinton. Sure, he was stupid to do it and lie about it, but he's a man after all. As a former Catholic, I had his back on the whole "I did not have sexual relations" thing. Any good Catholic school girl will tell what "sexual relations" means: A HOME RUN! INTERCOURSE! First, second, and third base don't count. Trust me, I spent a LOT of time on third base. The biggest lie he told was in 1994, before he was re-elected to a second term. Remember that MTV forum where a kid asked him, "boxers or briefs?" The President of the United States gave his sheepish answer and I remember thinking, "*Briefs*, my ASS! You *always* go commando, Bubba! Who do you think you're kidding?" The American people aren't *that* stupid.

Which is why I found myself getting so angry when self-righteous right-wing hypocrites started calling for his impeachment. He had been elected TWICE. We knew he had zipper issues and we didn't care. Maybe the 22 million new jobs he created seemed more important to people. Go figure.

I was the only national radio host who defended Bill Clinton. This is also because, at the time, I was also the ONLY liberal with a national talk radio show. And, as I said over and over at the time, on my show, and on Larry King's, and to Matt Lauer on the Today show: "I voted for him as my president, not as my husband." Not that the husband thing was an option for me, but I TOTALLY understood the point about "We call it a private life because it's supposed to be, oh, what's that word again...PRIVATE!!" I've always said that I lost my "political virginity" to Bill Clinton. And it's true.

But as much as I still love him, that's as close as he's gonna get. Although I've known many women, and even some straight men, who've said: "Oh, I would TOTALLY fuck Bill Clinton." Sorry, Bubba, the only Big Dog that's ever getting into bed with me is one of my Great Pyrenees, Max or Fred.

WINE! WHINE! WINE!

"I'd rather have a bottle in front of me than a frontal lobotomy." (This is a quote often attributed to the great Dorothy Parker, but I like to think of it as originating with George W. Bush, who proved that both things are possible.)

Don't lie to me. This is the chapter you've been waiting for, *A Brief History of My Time in a Bottle*. It contains the perfectly-fermented essence of Mama's philosophy of life. I grant you that it's not for everyone. If you're in middle school or rehab, I strongly urge you to skip this section. Or resell the book for drinking money. But if you're a red-wine blooded American like me, let me sum it up for you as clearly as I can: there's no such thing as a drinking *problem*. There is only a drinking *solution*.

My personal solution is wine, with a little whine on the side.

Let me make one thing clear from the outset. Mama does not advocate anyone becoming an actual drunk. Partly because I am a caring individual who does not wish on anyone a struggle with substance abuse, and partly because I hate it when AA people get all "programmy" with me—as much for their sake as for my own. I'm like a recovery third rail and should be avoided at all costs. I'm the *anti-sponsor.* They should have a Stephanie Miller poster up in every church basement in the country so everyone knows to steer clear.

Have you ever had someone try to make amends with you for something a thousand years after whatever the fuck it was they think they did to you that you can't even remember now because you were probably drunk too? I have. It was the *worst!* I had an old radio cohort who, for some bizarre reason, was really jealous of me. Even at the time I couldn't imagine what in the world there was to be jealous of, since my only bankable radio talent was my ability to deliver traffic reports while doing a Katharine Hepburn impression. Nevertheless, this guy was really mean to me daily, spreading malicious gossip that I made up overturned tractor-trailer alerts and that I had actually stolen my Katharine Hepburn impression from Rich Little. Oh, yeah, and he would call me a cunt. To my face, to anyone who would listen, he would call me a cunt.

That was something new and disturbing to my virginal ears at the time, unlike now, when I hear it almost as often as "Good morning!" from many of my right-wing, er, *"fans."*

Years later, I was at a radio convention, which is basically summer camp for talk show geeks, and he approached me with this wide smile, as if he was relieved to see me. I barely recognized him; he looked like he'd had radical surgery to remove his rage gland. He came up reeeeeal close and, in an octave that could have been helium-induced, earnestly blurted out, "I just want to tell you that I'm truly sorry."

"Um…it's okay," I said. "Don't worry about it." It had been 20 years. I had absolutely no clue what he was talking about.

He leaned in even closer (if he were any closer, he would actually have been *inside* me like the creature poking out of that guy in *Alien*) and, in classic boring-again sobriety, implored me to *hear* him. "No, listen. I'm really, *really* sorry."

Say it with me: *AWKWARD!*

"No, it was nothing," I said, trying desperately—and unsuccessfully—to remember what he was trying to apologize for having done to me. (By the way, this is how Mama handles awkward moments, by making the entire situation about me.)

"Stephanie, no, I'm *genuinely* sorry." He was trying very hard at this. I was trying very hard to become invisible.

"I drank back then," he said, his eyes welling up. "I was full of anger. My life was terrible. I said terrible things about you. I'm much better now, I'm in recovery. I'm on Step 9— making amends. I *have* to be able to apologize to you."

I wouldn't let him. Fuck that noise! I was too hungover for noise anyway. Call it Catholic guilt or the fact that after this conversation I knew I was going to swig a goblet of Bordeaux the size of my head, but I shot right back, "Nope. Absolutely not. It was all totally my fault. I was so insecure back then, I'm sure I was a complete bitch. It really wasn't you, it was me. You don't have any reason to make anything up to me."

He was beginning to become anxious. "No, Stephanie, you see, I *have* to do this. It's one of the steps."

"Nuh-uh. I was the one at fault. *You* were only telling everybody the truth. I remember everything," I lied. "You helped me out a lot. I learned that I couldn't treat people that way. I'm so sorry."

"No, please, I'm sorry."

"Nope. I can't let you take the blame. I'm sorry."

"This is part of my recovery, please let me apologize…"

We went back and forth like this for quite a while until finally I said, "Sorry, your apology is simply not accepted here," and walked away.

I suppose I should feel terrible about it. But I don't. I would gladly have helped him make a list of everyone else he'd harmed or taken his personal inventory, but apologies just make me too uncomfortable.

If he's out there reading this, it's STILL my fault. Sorry. (See what I did there?)

I am not a drunk, nor should you be. However, *drinking* is something else again. Drinking is what smart, sexy, sophisticated people do to forget that when they're *not* drunk, they're dumb, homely, and clumsy.

The whine chaser sometimes comes in the form of e-mails and texts from me the next day: "Ooh, I'm really sorry for saying (INSERT OVERLY SENTIMENTAL OR UTTERLY INAPPROPRIATE COMMENT HERE) last night. I got run over by the wine truck *again*. By the way, what *DID* I say?" It's not that I'm shy, but a few sips at the start of an evening can really make my social engine hum. It's a responsibility I take very seriously. I'm not really drinking for myself as much for everybody else. Because of me, several parties have gone from lackluster to legendary. I've put hosts on the map.

Some people get preachy and say, "Wine doesn't help." I always say "What are you a fucking MORON? Of course, it does. It helps a *lot.*" There is absolutely nothing in life that can't be achieved if you have the right amount to drink. There's no mountain that can't be climbed (St. Bernard's have that keg around their neck for a good reason), no desert that can't be crossed (my mirage is a *bottle*, not a body of water), and no potential date that can't be seen as attractive, especially after last call.

I come by my love of wine honestly. I have 50% Polish blood, 25% German blood and the remaining 25% is Chardonnay. Okay, the other 25% is actually *Irish*, but isn't that the same thing? All of it 100% pure Catholic. Among my earliest memories is the priest offering "the blood of Christ." I'd watch my neighbors as they would sip the chalice from my pew and say "Eww, gross!" Of course, that was when I was still just a *practicing* Catholic. Eventually, I became so good at it I turned professional and now I don't need to practice anymore.

I may not subscribe to much of the official doctrine any more, but from a very young age you learn that drinking is the very first miracle. It's right there in the New Testament, no matter how you choose to interpret it. Jesus, Mary, and the disciples are attending the Wedding at Cana and Mary says to Jesus, "They have no wine," a moment that always rang true for me: seriously, has there ever been a wedding where some old lady guest doesn't have a complaint? ("These canapés are dry!" "The music's too loud!" "Doesn't she know the groom's a queer?") So what does Mary's son do? Turns water into wine and everybody's thrilled. Who wouldn't prefer that to a Crate & Barrel gift certificate? The master of the banquet says to the groom, "Every man brings out the choice wine first and then the poorer wine after the guests have had too much to drink; but thou has kept the good wine until now." Jesus solved the wine problem and made the groom look good in the process. See...a wine *solution*.

Truthfully, I was never a big drinker growing up. I didn't graduate from baby bottle to bourbon bottle, despite my Catholic upbringing. Hard liquor, like the vodka my dad drank with his "silver bullets," makes me sick. On those very rare occasions when I have had a sweet cocktail, projectile vomiting is my revenge of choice on the person who poured it. I won't turn it down, mind you, but I always give the bartender fair warning: *"You're OUT of wine? Really?! Okay, then give me the fucking green appletini and step away from the bar, motherfucker!"* I'm no expert in Aramaic, but those words were not an option for Jesus, I'm guessing.

When I was a teenager, there was a bar we used to go in Lockport called The Friar where they'd serve *anybody* wine in exchange for cash, even if you looked like you were still in kindergarten. The added allure of that upstanding establishment was they'd also throw in free peanuts. Then you could toss the shells on the floor, which was even more exciting for our fake I.D. crowd—underage drinking *and* littering! Buffalo in the 70's was a wide-open town! Sin City! Vegas on the Erie.

My taste back then ran towards Riunite on ice ("How nice!") as well as such *Wine Advocate* favorites as MD20/20, Strawberry Ripple and, other brands known to the public mostly from episodes of "Sanford and Son." Doug, my boyfriend at the time, if you could call him that, broadened my palate considerably, like a screw-top sommelier, introducing me to a syrupy Lambrusco, our truly awful ass-nosed, locally-harvested Lake Niagara wine, and Blue Nun Liebfraumilch, which was like the Chateaux Lafite of wines available for less than four dollars. Doug was cute and funny and, given our fumbling, inept efforts to be sinful we needed all the inhibition-inhibitors we could get our hands on. At 14 or 15, it's all about quantity. He was very sweet to me and had tight curly locks like Greg Brady that looked a lot like pubic hair. When we were out drinking, I scratched his head sometimes and I think he was imagining I was scratching his balls in public. I had my first orgasm with Doug, which I thought at the time was a seizure. We were making out in the front seat of his car and I ended up on top of him. I had decreed that if we were in the back seat, I would be a slut. But I was ONLY a front seat slut, just so we're all clear on that.

Most of the time it was just me and the girls. It was far better to be caught by the nuns with a bottle than a boy (bottles they understood). Since we all took it as a tenet of the faith, my entire Catholic high school class was always fairly inebriated. My girlfriends and I would drink Old Vienna splits down by the railroad tracks. Our "gang" consisted of the two O'Neill girls—Babe (my best frenemy), and her cousin, Molly and our other friend, Jackie Maloney. It was like a bad "Girls Gone Wild" video. No exposed tits, just a bunch of Catholic school girls in plaid uniforms giggling together over our illicit beer. Yes, I know that "Catholic school girls in plaid uniforms" is a really hot porn search term, we'd actually have been more useful for any teenage boy wanting to *delay* orgasm, if not put it off altogether.

I was such a lightweight at that point in my young drinking life I'd usually have to stop at one glass of Reuniti or the mental boat would begin to drift away from the dock. To me the MD20/20 (also known as "bum wine") was really hitting it hard. I wasn't a serious wine drinker back then because I knew I was too young and I was still trying hard to be a *good* Catholic girl. I never missed class. I never missed sports practice. I never missed anything. In fact, I was such a goody-goody, I was voted "Best Brown Nose" in my high school.

I remember one day in Spanish class, I made Babe O'Neill laugh and Mr. Donnelly, our testy teacher, yelled at her for being disruptive. "Por favor, Señor Dillon," Babe said in a Spanish accent that was the equivalent of Ricky Ricardo's English, "It was Stephanie! She was the one who made me laugh!" He looked at her coldly and said, "Well, Señorita O'Neill, if you had *her* grades, maybe *you'd* have something to laugh about." This immediately increased Babe's already white hot resentment of me by a thousand more degrees. She love/hated me all the way through high school. *Que buena!*

Looking back on my teenage drinking days now, I realize that I got away with a lot of shit simply because by the time my brother and I arrived on the scene, my parents were a lot older—almost two decades—than they were when our sisters were growing up. They went to bed much earlier when Bill and I were teens, so they were much more permissive than they had been with Libby and Mary. (Luck of the draw, girls!)

There was no checking in, no interrogations of where I was or if there were boys. With me they'd just ask, "Oh Stephanie, what time did you come in last night?" And I'd reply, innocently twisting one of my curls, "What time did *you* go to bed?"

"We went to bed at eight," and like a lightning-round contestant, I'd buzz in with "8:30!! I got home at 8:30!" Then, ever the good girl, I'd add, "I was really quiet, though, because I didn't want to wake up you and dad." At this point my curl was completely twirled around my finger, as was my mother. She would just nod and say, "That's nice, dear." Sorry, sisters, the times had a'changed.

Ironically, whenever we had these conversations, my mother was usually deeply preoccupied with preparing for the cocktail hour and my father's imminent return from the office. God bless them, my parents were characters right out of "Mad Men." Like clockwork, my father would come home every day by 5:00 PM and my mother would have his highball poured and out waiting for him. And, as it was for most of the men of my dad's generation, that was simply the way things were supposed to be. The Pope was on his golden throne, the sun rose in the east, and the vodka Martini was always on the TV tray.

Did I mention that I was 25% Chardonnay?

As I said before, I've basically avoided spirits other than wine and beer all my life, but college is the time for bold experimentation with new friends from diverse backgrounds.

Even at that I was completely lame. Here I'd moved across the country to USC to live in Los Angeles, break into show-biz, and become the next Carol Burnett—or Carol Channing, at least. Freshman year, my roommate, Tina (who grew up in New York City), was Jewish. I'd only known Catholics my entire life, so when Tina danced around our tiny uni-dorm room (which cost my father hundreds of dollars per square foot) imitating Barbra Streisand, I had no idea what she was doing. It wasn't until years later, not until most everyone in my life was Jewish, or gay, or both, that I realized that Barbra adoration, is, along with Zionism and retiring to Fort Lauderdale, part of the definition of Modern American Judaism. And the gay Jews? Well, enough said.

But I knew nothing of this back then. I mentioned something about "Jewishness" to my best male friend, David, and when he said he, too, was Jewish I actually asked, "What *is* that? Is that a religion or a nationality or what?" He looked at me like I had three heads—which I guess I did; all of them equally clueless. Tina didn't drink at all during that first year in college, so neither did I. That was a Jewish thing, too, apparently. The WASPs and Catholics could really put it away (it's in the Bible!), but Tina confessed that even a few stealthy nips of Mogen David at a bar mitzvah would put her under the table. It would have helped a lot if I had been drinking, since Tina's Streisand impression was horrifically bad, and the twin tortures of sobriety and her painfully off-key "People" made my freshman year seem fucking *endless*. People whose roommates sing "People" are the unluckiest people in the world.

Sophomore year, I'd changed roommates and began expanding my horizons...a little. One night, while most of my friends were in their rooms tripping out on 'shrooms and debating the subtle but profound meaning of "Stairway to Heaven," I brazenly guzzled down a couple of grasshoppers (the drink, not the insect), piled into the car with my new roommate Annie and a couple of other friends to go see a midnight showing of "The Rocky Horror Picture Show." The low-point of my "high" that night was throwing up out of the car window on the freeway, wildly hurling chunks over four lanes of traffic. (Only later would I perfect my projectile vomiting to its current deadly accuracy.)

I know what you're thinking: a bunch of college students, stuffed into a beater car going to see "Rocky Horror"—it's as if we'd flipped to a random page in the The Big Book of College Fun, 1980 edition. I was part of that unattractive generation sandwiched between the Free Love Baby Boomers and the sourpuss slackers of Generation X. I was much too much of a good girl to be a punk, so instead of transgression, I settled for...*hijinks*. Always Mary Ann, never Ginger.

Because we'd already been drinking back at the dorm, someone thought it would be a good idea to stop and buy a bottle breath-freshening green crème de menthe at the liquor store. I had yet to discover that my metabolism falls right in the middle of the booze-o-meter: if Dad's "silver bullets" are on one end, and crème de menthe is on the other, six or seven glasses of medium-dry, full-bodied-but-not-too-fruity wine is my sweet spot.

A grasshopper is a vile drink—it goes down looking green as Linda Blair's breakfast, and its coloring doesn't improve on the way back out. All I can remember about that night now was thinking that the theater entrance, beneath the shelter of the marquis, looked like a really good place to take a nap. I had never been drunk enough to know that you can switch instantaneously from life of the party to Rocky Horror road kill. I only vaguely recall curling up in front of the theater and mumbling to the people stepping over me, "Will you save me a seat? I'll be right in." I was in my own personal Time Warp. Looking back, it may well have marked my first political jump to the Left.

Years later, I went to see "The Rocky Horror Picture Show" *without* drinking and I finally got to throw rice at the screen, as sober people will do.

Other than the infamous "Grasshopper Incident," I don't remember ever getting super drunk in college either. I was in Theater Arts and I really only drank at cast parties on the weekend following the run of the play. Then, after college, I didn't really drink at all. I like to think of those as my exercise/bulimia years trying to be an actress. My USC classmates—Ally Sheedy, Forrest Whitaker, Eric Stoltz, Anthony "ER" Edwards, Tate Donovan (he dated Jennifer Aniston!)—were all in the fancy Bachelor of Fine Arts theater program, while I was in the more "well-rounded" BA program that I thought would lead to stardom and wild success. Sadly, I was mistaken. Virtually ALL of my contemporaries are *way* more successful than I am.

With tons of makeup, I was the stunningly convincing "Grandmother" in the Edward Albee classic play "The American Dream." John Blankenship, the legendary USC acting teacher, called it the "best example of comedic age-acting" he had ever seen. My college career high point came during a summer production of Wendy Wasserstein's wonderful play "Uncommon Women and Others," in which I played Holly, a character described as:

> *Hair disheveled, yet well cut. She wears expensive clothes that don't quite match, not because she doesn't know what matches, but because she doesn't want to try too hard. That would be too embarrassing. A relief for many years on the adage "If she lost twenty pounds she'd be a very pretty girl, and if she worked, she'd do very well," Holly devised a strong moral code of warmth for those you love and wit for those you're scared of.*

Holy shit: not much of a stretch! Add "drinks a little to compensate for crazy radio lifestyle" and that's pretty much the woman I've become.

Playing Holly coincided with the *lowest*-point of what would become a very flat line on a graph of acting career low-points. It was during the run of "Uncommon Women" that I had to take a job as the camp counselor/bus driver for a Los Angeles summer camp for children disabled by over-privilege. I did it cheerfully, though, climbing behind the wheel every day humming "Hello, world, here's a song that we're singin'," and pretending I was Laurie Partridge, or pretending I was sleeping with Laurie Partridge—one of those two. But it became clear pretty quickly that a whole lotta lovin' was not what *my* bus was bringin'. After the little Fauntleroys had tuckered themselves out horseback riding, playing tennis, and selling junk bonds, they all boarded the bus holding little plastic bags with goldfish they'd been given as presents by the camp. Blessed with the skills of most first-time uncertified bus drivers, I kept running over curbs, pinballing that thing all the way home, causing the goldfish bags to bounce up and down on their precious laps. These poor rich kids (who could afford koi on their allowance money alone) kept screaming, "You're *killing* our goldfish!" First, and just for the record, no goldfish were ever injured by my driving. Second, and more important, this was a moment of awakening for me. I realized that for the first time in my life, I was the hired help, and I could be screamed at, just as their parents screamed at their gardeners and maids. You could feel the party lines hardening in their little minds. Entitlement doesn't fall far from the Republican tree.

One day toward the end of the season I pulled up to a boy who came all the way out to the curb to tell me, "I can't go to camp today. I have to go to Europe." Ok...Fuck you, Richie Rich! But who am I to judge? Not until you drive a mile in their parents' Porsches…

I did not by any means grow up deprived. (What's coming now, by the way, is a little whine on the side.) Dad was a lawyer, mom was a housewife, and we were secure; we had a nice house, even if was in a region of New York State that most resembled the Yukon. But it's hard to imagine now that the daughter of a candidate for Vice President of the United States—especially a Republican candidate—could have lived a life of relatively modest means. As I said, since I was only three, I don't remember much of the circus that was the losing-est Republican campaign of the century, by the popular vote, anyway. Going into politics then—and definitely for my parents—was a sacrifice, a calling, a service. And when the election was over, it was back to the law practice for my dad, to evenings at home looking at Walter Cronkite with a silver bullet waiting for him on the TV tray.

Today, devoting your life to politics is like becoming a reality show contestant. It's a win-win situation, where if you're elected you wield power and get chummy with lobbyists and multi-nationals, eventually land on a corporate board of directors, and get a book deal. And if you *don't* get the office you become a lobbyist or join the board of directors, and get a book deal. Washington itself becomes the career. The 113th Congress had the richest freshman class in American history, with a median net worth of $1,066,515—only about a million more dollars than the average American: A government of the poor, by the rich, for the rich… (Alright: whine over. Back to wine.)

For someone as devoted to the greatness of the grape as I am now, you're probably wondering why it took me so long to get started—I mean *really* started. That's because, as with most of the big initiations in life, it was connected to romance. I didn't start drinking much until I met my first long term love, Laurie, in the late nineties. Laurie (no relation to Laurie Partridge) was the one who introduced me to really good wine—the kind of wine whose flavor profile can't be unfavorably compared to a 7-Eleven Slurpee.

I was not out yet, but I was dating. Laurie and I arranged to meet for our first date at a bar in West Hollywood. I arrived early and already had a glass wine in front of me when Laurie walked in. She looked beautiful but eyed my wine suspiciously as she coolly informed me that she had sworn to never go out with *anyone* who drank white Zinfandel. I, of course, immediately did a spit take with my white Zinfandel, and yelled at the bartender, "This isn't what I asked for!" when, in fact, I'd requested it specifically by brand name and then tried to bargain him down. In any case, it was love at last white. Laurie, the oenophile, wiped the Zin off her chin and smiled sweetly at me. Score!

Laurie's and my relationship flourished at end of the Clinton Administration, just as the Monica Lewinsky-impeachment crisis was playing out in all its right-wing fueled, blood lust fever. We watched in anger and we drank in solidarity with Our Boy Bill. Remember when Newt Gingrich said how he started his affair with Calista because of "how passionately [he] felt about this country?" Just like Newt, Laurie and I also loved our country so much that we felt it was our patriotic duty to drink our way through the American Horror Picture Show of impeachment. And we threw a lot more than rice at the television screen. "Mazel tov!" we shouted as we hurled our empty wine glasses at Ken Starr's smug ass face. After all, what's a little shattered glass when the Constitution is at stake?

Liberal drinking is a political science that Mama has spent her adult lifetime studying carefully. I believe that strategic inebriation is every good citizen's civic duty. Take the Clinton impeachment. For Laurie and me, the case against Bill turned into many cases of Pinot Noir for us. Liberals need to drink more, not less. A stiff drink equals a stiff spine. Dicks, I'm told, are another matter entirely.

The 2000 Florida recount was a perfect example of how liberals don't fight as tough and effectively as conservatives. I know some outraged Democrats who "protested" the Bush v. Gore decision by switching from screwdrivers to Bloody Marys. Lame! They stopped counting Gore votes and all we could think of to do was stop buying their fucking oranges.

I say hit them where it hurts. Rather than trying to win our argument on the facts—which they don't care about anyway—we should have just cut off Scalia's bar tab. "No more Chianti for you, Justice Mussolini!"

Instead, we were stuck with a "dry-drunk" president for eight years. Does anybody really believe that that W wasn't completely hammered throughout his entire presidency? Gimme a break. No sober person ever mangles the English language that badly. Read the following statements and ask yourself honestly, would you let this person drive your *car*, let alone your country?

- "Rarely is the question asked: Is our children learning?"

- "I am mindful not only of preserving executive powers for myself, but for predecessors as well."

- "I know the human being and fish can coexist peacefully."

- "I know how hard it is for you to put food on your family."

You want to know how we can really build a better America? Just force Tea Party Republicans to drink ONLY tea (instead of their usual Kool-Aid martinis). They'd jump ship quicker than you can say "Boston Harbor." If bat-shit crazy conservatives (I'm talking to *YOU*, Ted Nugent) were eighty-sixed by liberal bartenders everywhere, Fox News would go out of business overnight and every corporate CEO would join the Occupy movement just to get a beer and some weed. (Sorry, more whine.)

Okay, now that I've saved the country, let's get back to me. How long has it been? Five minutes, you say? It felt like an eternity. Let me just take a second to refill my glass…

I became a connoisseur of fine wine while I was with Laurie. Even though our relationship didn't last, we remain friends—and wine lovers—to this day. Even though wine drinking started as a part of sealing a romantic connection for me, it later evolved into salving the romantic pain of subsequent years. There's nothing more romantic than sharing a great bottle of wine with a great love. Or...a cheap bottle of wine with friends or dogs that are trying to help you get over that bitch...I mean great love.

Relationships invariably change you in ways you don't realize at the time. I think the only thing that saves me from being an alcoholic is Laurie's lasting influence on my taste in wine. Because of her, I'm now a total wine snob and there are wines I just *won't* drink. Fortunately for me and my liver, my professional mediocrity prevents me from regularly buying any bottle costing more than $30. I'm pretty much at a radio/cable celebrity level of drinking. If Kathy Griffin has the D-List to herself, I'm an E-Lister. Is there a Z-List? Jesus may have saved the choice wine for last. I save it for the nights I'm not buying. There are some wine aisles in the wine store I can't even *afford* to enter. They might as well be roped off with a bouncer. "Oh, *that's* the Diane Sawyer aisle. You can't go in *there*." (It was always fun to watch her stammering through election night coverage. Believe me Diane, I feel your pain. If I had to cut to George Will for commentary, I'd do exactly the same thing—especially if I had your salary.)

Counterintuitively, despite years of "Sex and the City" cosmos and Motley Crue Sunset Strip Jack Daniels binges, New York and Los Angeles, the cities I've spent most of my life in, don't even rank among the most crocked cities in the country. Putting on their sternest looks and waving their "American Gothic" pitchforks in our faces, Republicans would like you to believe that New York and Los Angeles are hotbeds of liquored-up liberals, but according to the Daily Beast's invaluable list of the Top 25 Drunkest Cities in the United States, they don't even make the cut:

1) Boston (20.1% of its residents were determined to be "binge-drinkers")
2) Norfolk, Va.
3) Milwaukee
4) Charleston, S.C.
5) Austin, Texas
6) Hartford-New Haven, Conn.
7) New Orleans
8) Chicago
9) Washington, D.C.
10) Providence, R.I.
11) Minneapolis-St. Paul
12) Omaha, Neb.
13) Baltimore
14) Springfield, Mass.
15) Denver
16) Baton Rouge, La.
17) Reno, Nev.
18) San Francisco
19) Philadelphia
20) Fargo, N.D.
21) Las Vegas
22) Buffalo, N.Y.
23) St. Louis
24) Cleveland
25) Burlington, Vt.

Mama's personal theory is that Boston was Number #1 in 2012 because they'd spent the entire year drinking heavily at the prospect of their former governor Mitt Romney becoming president. The irony is that Romneycare covers the cost of their liver transplants. How proud is Mama, though, that her native Buffalo made the list: #22 (with a Silver Bullet!). Of all the cities in America, even Pittsburgh. Buffalo's right where it should be, immediately behind its

Sister Sin City, Las Vegas. I like to think Dad would be proud too.

I sometimes wonder what my life would have been like if I'd been raised in one of the more puritanical religions: Mormonism, Islam. It's altogether possible I might be much more successful than I am. Not that Catholicism didn't have its restrictions, it's just that wine wasn't one of them. Authoritarian religions are reliably (and hypocritically) assholic about telling you what you can do with your body *after* the drinking.

If I'd been raised into a successful Scientology family, can you imagine the wine cellar I'd have? Tom Cruise can spend millions on the things he loves—motorcycles, planes, divorces. I'd build one of those humidity-and-temperature-controlled walk-in wine cellars and have my collection itemized by nationality, region, grape, vintage, and a pairing chart dictating the best bottle to pour depending on which pundit is screaming at you. I'd probably put a couch down there, a TV, a popcorn maker...again, I'm beginning to wonder if my business partner isn't right. If I ever became a Republican, I could afford to drink like one. You see, I live alone, in a nice home in Hollywood, like Norma Desmond in "Sunset Boulevard," who was played by Gloria Swanson (coincidentally one of the first Hollywood celebrities to flirt with Scientology). Like Norma, I rarely leave my house. Like her, I should get a driver, because *my* Max is a dog and doesn't drive. He DOES retrieve my fake fan mail, though, and help me fish the dead screenwriters out of my pool. So I mostly stay inside; my only drinking companions are my handsome and romantic Great Pyrenees dogs. As it happens, they prefer water, but I don't judge them and they don't judge me. Dogs are a drinker's best friend.

Listeners understandably get confused by my ability to drink and do my show coherently the next day. I always say I'm not *actually* a drunk, I just play one on the radio. They still don't believe me. As all my friends will tell you when asked, "Is Stephanie a violent drinker?" "No." "Is she a loud, shouty drinker?" "No." "Is she a *sleepy* drinker? Absolutely!"

Let me explain my so-called life to you. I have to wake up at the crack of *ass* (no, it's not even dawn when I start my commute, it's ass. And by my commute I mean stumbling down three staircases to my home studio) So for me it's simply a matter of adjusting the clock and drinking during daylight hours. Most normal Americans wake up for work at 7, take 5PM as the unofficial starting gun of the cocktail hour, drink until bed around 11:30, try fumbling around with their significant other in front of Jimmy Fallon, and wind up falling asleep four minutes later in the middle of his third Kardashian joke. Don't lie—this sounds familiar, right?

Adjust for a day in Morning Drive radio. My work doesn't stop when I get off the air at 9:00 AM. That's when my producer, Chris, and I start to monitor the world of cable news, talk radio, and wingnut websites for the best nuggets of illogic beamed straight to earth from Right Wing World. If I had that fantasy wine cellar, I'd pull out a crisp, frizzante white for Megyn Kelly; something dry, light-bodied for Laura Ingraham; a big-nosed red with a lot of barnyard for Michael Savage; and, for Limbaugh, whatever has the highest alcohol content. As I told you at the beginning of this book, I never actually get to see a Fallon monologue or prime time shows when they air, or even a sunset, for that matter, but I do have the mischievous pleasure of starting wine at 3, so my buzz coincides perfectly with the appearance of the Fox News Romulan, Shepard Smith. Somewhere in there I try and remember to eat. By 6 o'clock, I'm in my pajamas, brushing my teeth, and eyeing my pillow with the fierce physical desire Sean Hannity has for his mirror.

My income being what it is (I'm telling you, liberal talk really *is* cheap), I pundit-pair with whatever it is I have on hand, but I have never returned to the days of Blue Nun and Riunite. Despite the strenuous, blurry afternoons of conservative assaults—"reverse racism," "welfare loafers," and "the Plan B president"—ends with a sleep of the angels. By 7 PM (or as we call it, stupid o'clock) you can find me curled up with Max and Fred until, at exactly insane o'clock, when they lick my face to get me up, and the whole process starts again.

This is not a routine I would wish upon anybody, and I only suffer it out of love—for my listeners and for my country. But seriously kids, do not try this at home. I frequently get callers to my show that sound like they're completely in the bag by 6:30 AM. They always ask the same question: "Shtephanie, wassh your shecret? I mean…I mean, like…you know what I'm ashking is…how do you drank so much and keep FUNKTIONING?"

My diction is perfect, as is my timing. "Functioning?!" I exclaim through a mild hangover. "Drinking is how Mama does her *best* functioning, baby!" By this point the caller has passed out, but my sober listeners tell me they are tremendously impressed. I know this because they repeatedly and lovingly send me *cases* of box wine.

This isn't to say that there aren't some health concerns associated with daily drinking. When I last gave a blood sample, the lab technician asked me if it was oaked or un-oaked, then they swirled around the vial and sniffed. I've never heard a word about my cholesterol, but I do know that my blood contains strong notes of stone fruit, licorice, black currant, and pencil shavings, has a startling acidity, and a surprisingly pleasant mouthfeel. I've always been very concerned about my mouthfeel—a fact I make sure to in-clude in my online dating profiles. My doctor called and immediately advised me to stop drinking. I thanked her, hung up and poured myself a glass of Chardonnay. Mama doesn't like bad news without her medicine. Oh, and I also switched doctors.

Should I ever get off this morning radio treadmill—or get a show that airs at a civilized time of day—maybe I'll cut down. For a year I moved to New York, where you can get anywhere by subway, cab or by foot. New Yorkers never have to drive, so they can get as drunk as they want. That's something that always baffles New Yorkers who come to LA: since in LA you always have to drive 45 minutes to get everywhere, how in the world do you have a drinking life? Pay attention, people, this is why God invented Uber!! Now, I'm back in LA and as the song goes: "It never rains in Southern California, but girl don't they warn ya', the wine pours, man it pours!" Or at least that's how *I* remem-ber the lyrics.

Here's the good news: at least I've FINALLY figured out what I'm really best at. As it turns out, it's drinking AND swearing. I now do a weekly raunchy, drunken, FCC-free version of my radio show with some of my best comedy buddies, and the "Best of Stephanie Miller's Happy Hour Podcast, Volume 1" is, as I write, the Number One comedy album in America on Amazon, Itunes, and Google Play with 5 star reviews on all three! Yes, at long last I've figured out the color of my parachute, and as it happens, it's the color of a nice pinot noir. I'm doing it on my own. And if I ever figure out who moved my cheese in Hollywood, I'm going to throw a nice big, buttery chardonnay in their fucking face!

Author's postscript: I just woke up at the Betty Ford Center, which is where overindulgent liberals go to be cared for by the ghosts of Republican first ladies.

MY LIFE OF CRIME

I guess I should mention at some point, in advance of my inevitable presidential run, that I've been arrested. Nailed, nabbed, pinched, busted—- just like George W. Bush, and like him it involved drinking. It certainly didn't stop him from getting elected and going on to wreck the country, and most of the free world (much as I would), but it does make you think that his eventual sobriety probably wasn't such a good idea. There, that's out of the way. I just vetted myself right in front of you.

I was nineteen and a sophomore at USC, the University of Southern California. The drinking age in New York State, where I grew up, in Lockport, up the transit from Cheektowaga, was 18. Though my memory is hazy, I'm pretty sure our high school mascot was a giant Gennesee cream ale empty. In California, however, you had to be 21, which slowed things down on campus, but just a bit. However, there was one liquor store that was notorious for being a little "loose," shall we say, with the whole "carding minors" thing. If you were tall enough to reach the cash slot in the bullet-proof glass, you were good to go. My roommate Loni, who looked like she was 12, begged me (who, apparently, looked 50) to go buy her a six-pack of light beer. In Los Angeles you've got to watch those empty calories.

I didn't want to do it. I was boy-crazy and actually had a date that night. By the way, if the "boyfriend thing" just threw you off, read the chapters in order people! I turned out to be a big Lez, don't make me pull this book over! But, of course my liberal tendencies were always to help those in need until they were old enough to help themselves, including my roommate Loni, and I said OK.

What then should have been the simplest petty crime in the world went terribly, terribly wrong. I go in to buy the beer and actually got carded. I could probably have purchased an assault weapon, but I was deemed by the state unfit to handle half a dozen bottles of Coors Light. The guy next to me, spotting my distress, said, "I'll buy it for you."

My first big mistake, listening to men. I said, "OK!"

CUT TO: store exterior, screeching tires, klieg lights, police sirens. On the megaphone, a harsh voice blared, "Up against the wall and spread 'em!" (which, later in life, and with candles, I would consider the end of a successful evening). Yes, I got caught in a sting operation, and there was no Robert Redford or Paul Newman anywhere to be found.

I got handcuffed with my enabler, and thrown in the back of a police car. I remember the drive to the station, asking him "Have you ever been arrested before?" "Oh, yeah," he said. "Rape, robbery, carrying a concealed weapon...."

So I get hauled down to the police station for the ugliest mug shot ever taken, I asked for something kind of kicky like Patty Hearst, but he went more for straight-up Squeaky Fromme, complete with the "Oh God, my dad's gonna kill me!" snot running down my face. I was talking to some of the other "perps" while I was handcuffed on the bench waiting for booking, making conversation as you do. Niceties such as, "Whose urine do you think we're smelling?" and "If you had any more teardrop tattoos on your face, you'd look just like a rainforest!" I kept asking, "What are *you* in for?" and hearing answers I really didn't want to... murder, mayhem, you know, the usual. It's Saturday night in Los Angeles. Gack.

So finally I "got out," as my fellow homeys say. Yes, I had to make that fateful call-of-shame to the Republican parents for bail money, the call every parent and child cherishes. Why do they never make AT&T commercials about that?

My dad hired a fancy Beverly Hills lawyer who was between Liz Taylor divorces and got my charge knocked down to "minor in possession," basically a traffic ticket.

Even that got expunged, because in those days everyone worried about what it would do to your "permanent record" and your future, if you ever wanted to have a successful life. Like W., I learned that the real secret to achieving success in life was to be a white kid with powerful parents. Little did my dad know that I would grow up to be a fart joke comedian whose resume requires some really stupid shit done as a college idiot.

But God bless my daddy who said, "God damn it, that was the most expensive six-pack I ever bought!" and who got that ugly-ass mug shot disappeared into the cornfield forever. I love you, Dad...sorry I was such a pain in the ass.

And lesson learned: I don't drink beer anymore. Please pass the corkscrew.

After my "minor in possession of alcohol" bust in college, I decided to lay low for about thirty years, like many serial killers and other hardened criminals, just to throw the cops off my trail. When I next struck again, at age 51, with my "dog off a leash" ticket, they never saw it coming. Come and get me, coppers, you'll never take me alive! *Attica! Attica!*

Yes, on a typically cloudless California day, I hit again—and this time it was in broad daylight. As I do every day, I took my beloved Great Pyrenees dogs, Max and Fred (each of whom is bigger than the trees they mark), hiking in LA's famous Griffith Park. For those of you who've never been there, it's a vast expanse of wooded land and hilly trails, right in the heart of our giant metropolis. It's famous for the Observatory at the top (where James Dean got into that classic knife fight in "Rebel Without a Cause") and for the many gay trysts that used to take place there illicitly until LGBT people were finally allowed to come out of the shrubs.

I, for one, have never had sex in a public place. This is largely because I rarely have sex in private places, so the idea has never even occurred to me.

No, my crime was not indecent exposure or public fornication. (God, I wish. Bucket list!)

My crime, my act of unspeakable evil on an unsuspecting populace, was to let my dogs off the leash. And you know what? I'd do it again. Everybody at Goldman Sachs goes free and makes millions; I get nailed by a park ranger with a quota. Where's the *justice*?!

And once again, I was caught in a sting operation. This is how it all went down: I saw the ranger coming toward me in time to get Max back on the leash. But Fred was out of my reach and the ranger knew it. He smiled at me with a look that said, "It's over, Miller. We've got you dead to rights." I shot him back a look that said, "Damn. I'm going to be late for cocktail hour." I briefly considered making a run for it until I realized that I wasn't Patrick Swayze in "Point Break," but more like Jessica Tandy in "Driving Miss Daisy." And that fucking Morgan Freeman is NEVER around when you need him.

Then the ranger handcuffed me to a tree and I started screaming wildly about "police brutality." OK, OK. What *actually* happened is that his pen ran out of ink while he was writing me the ticket and I loaned him mine. You remember: Liberal=Helper.

Smiling my sweetest smile I asked him if there wasn't some other way we could take care of this. He said. "Sure, lady. You can put your dog on the leash next time."

Turns out that I actually had to go to court...criminal court...downtown. On Christmas Eve.

So there I am, waiting for the judge to hear my case with, let's just say, a *diverse*...assortment of people with an amazing assortment of hair colors and body odors. I sat there for an hour hearing a variety of cases from domestic violence, to a homeless guy with an assault charge that they brought in to a glass cage in the court already wearing a prison jumpsuit and handcuffs, to a surprising amount of people who had jumped the turnstile to ride the subway without paying for a ticket. First of all, we have *subway trains* in LA? Who knew?!

I finally went up to the bailiff to ask why my case wasn't being called. He said, "You're still holding the sheet of paper you were supposed to put in the basket so your case *can* be called."

"Oh. Right. Sorry, I'm new at this." *It puts the paper in the basket, and the lotion on its arms, and back in the basket, or it gets the hose again.* Whatever, Rusty the Bailiff, just call my case, I've got shit to do.

The judge, who was older than the cast of *Cocoon*'s grandparents, finally called my name.

"Miss Miller?"

"Yes, your Honor." I stepped forward and there was a sudden stir in the courtroom. I could hear the whispers.

"It's that girl, you know the one on the radio."

"How do you know what she looks like? She's on the radio."

"It's her. I know. I saw her picture on the side of the bus. She thinks she's some sexy shit."

"Bony thing. She's got no ass."

This is now an out-of-body experience. I'm hearing all of this and realizing—with growing horror—that it will all be in the Los Angeles Times the next day. Meanwhile, the judge, who is stone cold deaf, doesn't hear a word of it.

The judge said, "So you were riding the train without paying for a ticket?" *Again*, with this shit? And, again, we have subway trains in LA? REALLY? I said, "No, I had my dog off a leash." He shuffled some papers around, seemingly as confused as I was that I actually had to be in fucking criminal court for this.

At this point, a couple of the prosecutors and other court employees recognized me and started giggling and waving frantically at me, asking if they could get pictures and autographs after this.

I am now officially in my own legal system Fellini film, *Stephtyricon*.

All this commotion confuses the judge even more, since he had no idea who I was, having been born several decades before Marconi invented radio. He said, "Well did your dog bite someone?"

I said, "No, he's really friendly." Judge Methuselah finally asked me if I could afford the fifty dollar fine, or whatever, and I said, "Yes." Thank God this story didn't end in debtor's prison, right?

I paid my fine, posed for pictures, and gave autographs to the court officers, one of whom said: "Wow, it's weird you're a liberal and it's all the prosecutors who are your fans!" I said, "Hey, I'm a *law and order* liberal!"

I am now, anyway.

Another lesson learned. Unless, of course, I decide to go nuts again in thirty years—who knows, I may fraudulently yell "BINGO!" or something. Criminals like me just *can't* be rehabilitated.

IT TAKES A VILLAGE OF RIGHT-WING IDIOTS

It's hysterical when people (other than my mother) say to me, "Stephanie, you've gotten SO liberal."

But it isn't me that's changed.

The current GOP leadership has gone so far off the map you can't find it with a GPS. (Well, I can't find anything with a GPS because I'm technologically impaired, but that'll be in my next book *"Anti-Social* Media!" It will explore my Amish-Luddite relationship with modern technology and will be written entirely in calligraphy, by candlelight, using only a quill pen.)

But seriously, can anyone drop a pin outside of Washington and find this version of the GOP anywhere?

People who used to be Goldwater-Miller conservatives are now barely in the center-right. Responsible Republicans like Richard Lugar, Mike Castle and Olympia Snowe were either defeated in primaries by Tea Party true-believers or forced into retirement in complete disgust with their own party. Liberals have been dragged to the middle just to keep the country from falling apart. Let's pretend we forgot that President Obama's "socialist" health care plan was originally Bob Dole's plan, the Heritage Foundation wrote it, and it was successfully used in socialist Massachusetts by socialist Republican presidential candidate Mitt Romney, for FUCK'S SAKE!

The Republican Party has changed so much since my dad and Goldwater's era that if they arrived in Washington, DC, today, they'd take one look at Tea Party crazies like Ted Cruz, Joni Ernst and Steve King and head for the nearest bar for vodka martinis, or as you'll remember that my Dad liked to call them, "silver bullets." In an illustration of the bi-partisan outreach of that era, my Dad always used to invite my best friend Tracey Richard's dad, Bob (who was our plumber and an avowed Democrat), over to fix things at the end of the day so they could enjoy silver bullets together. And if Grover Norquist had ever tried to tell my dad how to vote, he'd have said, "Excuse me, I signed a pledge to the Constitution of the United States of America, not to a man. And by the way, you have a Muppet name. Fuck off."

We're more than half a century down the road from their time, but even George W. Bush would be too liberal for the Insane Clown Posse that has completely taken over the modern GOP. If we're progressives, they're regressives. They say they just want to take us back to the Reagan era. And they continually evoke his sainted name as the only true conservative president we've ever had. Since they're a fact-free bunch who live in a world woven entirely out of whole cloth sprinkled with Roger Ailes fairy dust, Mama hates to burst their self-contained bubble (actually, it's my life's work), but Ronald FUCKING Reagan RAISED taxes 11 times. He raised the debt ceiling 18 times. He signed an amnesty provision for undocumented immigrants.

Even Mike Huckabee (who talks directly to God, so pay attention) admits "Ronald Reagan would have a very difficult, if not impossible, time being nominated in this atmosphere of the Republican Party." Make no mistake about it, if he showed up today Zombie Reagan would be teabagged right out of town. So would Barry Goldwater—those hipster black glasses would be knocked right into the next election cycle. (And Reagan would probably end up in that same bar getting snoggered with my dad and Barry.)

As Butch Cassidy said to the Sundance Kid about the posse that kept chasing them relentlessly, "Who *are* those guys?"

Mama's job is to answer that question for you. Let's open up the doors of the clown car and see who spills out, shall we? We'll take a peek at who they really are underneath the (very) white make-up, the fake red noses (John Boehner's is real), the big floppy shoes (Larry Craig found them especially helpful for his wide stance) and the mop of floppy orange hair (Carrot Top = Trump Top).

Ladies and Gentlemen, boys and girls—cast your eyes on the circus that is the Far Right Wing! Get your popcorn! Get your Republican talking points program! Your mind must be this small to go on this ride! But be warned, this show is not for the faint of heart. Pregnant women who don't wish to have a mandatory transvaginal probe should leave now. Your usher, former Virginia Governor/current inmate Bob McDonnell, now on work release, will show you to the nearest exit. And all unarmed children should stop by the NRA booth where that nice Mr. LaPierre will give you your very own gun. Pastel pink for girls or baby blue for boys. They'll even give a questioning kid a rainbow pistol. The only time they don't care if you're a Godless gay, is if you want a gun. Then it's praise the Lord and pass the fuckin' ammunition! Please don't worry if you once got into a playground fight or were ever sent to detention. There are no background checks here at the GOP circus!

Now, without further ado, let's introduce our class of GOP clowns. First one out of the car is House Speaker John— say it with me now—"BONER!!"

Bay-ner/Boner: WHATever. We all know it from grade school. "When two vowels go walking, the first one does the talking." I mean, c'mon, did Dick Armey change his name from Penis Airforce? OWN it, Boner.

There's a lot we know about him from his official biography. Thirteen term congressman from Ohio. Son of a barkeeper. One of twelve children. Yet Mama still has a lot of questions about the real man behind the tan. For example, do we know if John Boehner's dick is really as orange as the rest of his complexion? If you give him a hand-job will your fingers look you've been eating Cheetos all day? And why does a man cry that much when nothing heavy has fallen on him?

Boehner's not a man from my father's generation. As I mentioned earlier, when Barry Goldwater described my dad as "a man's man," he meant that he was a guy that other guys felt comfortable being around. Not in a Marcus Bachmann way. But John Boehner is just a weepy orange boner—his tears are an unwholesome emotional discharge.

Tragically, there's no penicillin strong enough to cure him. Someday, perhaps, they'll find a cure. Fortunately he'll be covered because of OBAMACARE. Orange may be the new black, but ironically *this* orange guy will be saved by a black president.

Stumbling next out of the clown car is Senate Majority Leader Mitch McConnell. I call him Yertle because he really looks like a turtle...it's the thick magnification of his glasses. Frankly, he just looks startled to be anywhere. He always says the President needs to slow down. Well, of course everything is always going too fast for a fucking TURTLE. He just wants to be back in his terrarium eating lettuce.

McConnell often speaks from the well of the Senate in a monotonous drawl that even the official secretary can't understand. He sounds like the evil spawn of Leon Redbone and Charlie Brown's teacher. This may be explained by the fact that he actually has no lips. With apologies to lipless people everywhere, Mama is mystified at how a person masticates food without having any lips. Senator McLipless is a miracle of modern science. Or at least he would be, if he actually believed in modern science. (I do owe him an apology, though. I used to call him Mitch McChinless until I realized that I was in error. In truth, he has an excess of chins that exist solely to distract people from his lack of lips. Sorry, Senator. It won't happen again.)

Following McConnell out of the clown car is former House Speaker Newt Gingrich. Newt's weight had depressed the tires so severely, that as soon as he stepped out, the car seemed to spring up into the air. And what's Newt doing? Oh, right, he's going right over to the audience and posing for pictures with anyone who'll pay him. But some of us get our Newtie for free. I got this picture when we were on the same flight from DC after President Obama's second inaugural. I don't know where Calista was. He must have divorced her somewhere between landing and baggage claim. Perhaps she developed one of those dry air coughs on the plane, and he decided to get while the getting was good.

(Photo courtesy of Stephanie Miller)

Wait a minute, who's that getting out of the clown car now? It's former Pennsylvania senator and failed presidential candidate Rick Santorum! There's a button on his lapel—what's it say? Can we bring the camera in for a closer look? "Santorum in 2016." Ah, Frothy, hope springs eternal, doesn't it?

While Santorum waves to the wildly cheering crowd (actually it's only the first row where his immediate family is sitting), I should explain how I was the first to give him the nickname "Frothy the Santorum" during the 2012 presidential primary campaign.

It started, of course when my friend, author and activist Dan Savage (who deserves a Nobel Prize for creating the "It Gets Better" campaign that has helped to save thousands of young LGBT kids from giving up on life) had the wickedly funny idea of holding a contest to find the most repulsive definition for "Santorum" his imaginative readers could come up with. The winner: "the frothy mixture of lube and fecal matter that is sometimes the byproduct of anal sex." Don't blame me. I'm only quoting here. (If you don't believe me, Google it yourself. Santorum once made that mistake and it hurt his tender feelings. I might feel a small pang of sympathy for Frothy, except for the fact that he was the sensitive soul who had previously compared gay relationships to "man on dog" or "man on child" sex.

Since Mama is so kid-friendly (provided they're at a safe distance), I decided to turn the name into a children's character, "Frothy the Santorum," a soiled and slippery snowman in a sweater vest. My audience loved it and it was perfect for the holidays when liberals declare our annual War on Christmas.

It's so good to see that Little Ricky is pulling his baggy pants back on and getting back into the clown ring! I've really missed him and his "miracle campaign." Frothy was the gift to liberal comedians that never stopped giving. On the eve of the Michigan primary that he had been poised to win, he said that President John F. Kennedy's speech about the separation of church and state made him want to "throw up." This devout Catholic then promptly proceeded to lose the Catholic vote for the first time. NO OTHER CATHOLIC CANDIDATE HAS EVER LOST THE CATHOLIC VOTE. Now I'm not a highly paid political consultant, but I am an ex-Catholic school girl (gone wild). And I'm just sayin' that the real Santorum miracle was that he wasn't mugged by a mob of angry nuns in Kalamazoo.

Ever since he melted down into a puddle in 2012, I've been saving two lumps of coal and a carrot in the fervent hope that he would somehow put himself back together again. You go Frothy!! As gay marriage is legalized all across the country, you keep facing the other way. The Dark Ages need someone to watch out for them while the rest of us move forward into reality.

Will Frothy really run again in 2016? Can any of us survive another Santorum surge? Or the giggle fit that ensues when Wolf Blitzer actually SAYS "The Santorum surge has led to a SPURT in fundraising"? Hey Wolf, it might be a good idea to spend a little more time with Mr. Google.

Although there is one change he may have to make the next time around. In 2012, Santorum's Secret Service code name was Petrus, in honor of St. Peter. I don't think that was too smart of Frothy. Just imagine this scene someday at the Pearly Gates:

"What's your name, my son?"

"Petrus."

St. Peter shakes his head and points downward, "You said all that crazy shit in MY name? Dude, you're riding the Santorum surge DOWNTOWN, my friend!"

Look, look, look! It's a man with a big push broom (and a mop—yecch) running over to clean up after Frothy! Don't you know who he is?! It's that "Republican Rapey guy" former Congressman Todd Akin of Missouri! You remember him don't you? Akin was the first in a growing line of Republicans who've said thing like "women's bodies have ways to shut themselves down after a legitimate rape." I know my vagina has magical superpowers; that just doesn't happen to be one of them. Fyi: mine tends to focus more on reversing the earth's rotation so that arch villains can't destroy major metropolises.

I learned more about women's reproductive systems from my high school health class than this idiot figured out after fathering six children, and I was taught by a nun whose only experience of sex was the warm feeling she got whenever that handsome Liberace tickled the ivories. In fact, I got my first big laugh as a prepubescent comedian-to-be when the nun informed us that crab lice were spread by swinging from hair to hair, and I blurted out, "Geronimo!"

Thank you. Try the veal, but not on Friday! Don't forget to tip your waiters, ladies!!

OK, can we all agree that even Clay Aiken knows more about women than Todd Akin? The idea that a super-powered va-jay-jay can create a special force field that blocks rapist sperm (while magically welcoming all the little Brad Pitt would-be zygotes) is so completely ridiculous that it would have been laughable if Akin had just been some average Joe-the-Plumber who didn't know anything about female plumbing. But, unfortunately, this asshat was the Republican nominee for ONE OUT OF ONLY A HUNDRED U.S. SENATE SEATS in the entire country, that small mostly men's club that once boasted James Monroe and John Quincy Adams as members. And just to add a little irony to the misogyny, he was also a member of the House Science Committee. Comforting thought, isn't it?

But back in 2012, Todd Akin was the perfect Republican candidate. He was dumb enough to say offensive things about women without caring and he was shameless enough to stay in the race when EVERYBODY, even Sarah "damn-the-lamestream-media full-speed-ahead" Palin begged him to drop out.

Not me. I shouted, "Go, Akin, go!" I would have said, "Drill, baby, drill!" but that would have only further encouraged the Rapey Republican crew.

Well, speaking of the Drill Baby, herself! Look who's getting out of the clown car now... Milfy McMooseburger. And, not surprisingly, she's got her whole family with her. Maybe it's because all of them are now more famous than she is. Even Levi. (Ouch. That must hurt a hockey mom/grifter.)

A few years ago all anyone wanted to talk about was Sarah Palin. Now her picture is on the side of milk cartons. She wasn't invited to the last GOP convention. When even someone as cynically soulless as Mitt Romney refuses to exploit you for political gain, you KNOW that you've definitely passed your expiration date.

Personally, I think it was her voice that finally wore America down to its last nerve.

I agree with the guy who called my radio show once when I played a Palin sound bite, and said "God, I think my balls just hit the back of my THROAT."

What IS it with that voice? Personally, I think it's like the sound of a band saw cutting through a bike frame. Or maybe it's more like the fingernails on Glenn Beck's old chalkboard. And have you noticed that as her poll numbers have gone down, the shrillness of her voice has actually gone UP? Soon only dogs will be able to hear her...glass will shatter, garage doors will fly up, women's tampons will come shooting out spontaneously.

I just hope she's saving some of that Fox money to use on therapy for her kids. They're going to need it. As I said at the beginning of this book, at least the Miller family had the heart not to exploit their abandoned wolf child for political gain (not that it would have helped them any).

"I am big," she can be heard saying. "It's Fox News that got small." Poor Alaska, it may be the largest state geographically, but there's still not enough square mileage to contain her ego. In a few years, the only place you'll see her name is in a Trivial Pursuit Advanced Edition, along with the name of Martin Van Buren's Vice President. But at this point, it's all about the money for the Palin clan. If the Palins thought they could get away with it (and they may yet), they'd have Trig tattooed with the Eli Lilly logo for a few hundred grand.

Do you remember in 2008 when she put all her kids on that big colored Partridge Family-on-acid bus with "SAR-AHPAC" emblazoned on it? She was prick-teasing report-ers all across the country about whether she was going to run for president or not. (That would be "not.")

And then, when a reporter had the temerity to actually take a picture of their publicity stunt, Piper (then only eleven and unaware that she was just part of the show) screamed at him: "THANKS FOR RUINING OUR VACATION!!!!"

Yikes. Mommy issues anyone? Fast forward to 2017. The scene is a psychiatrist's office in Wasilla:

"Anyway, doctor, one time, my Mom told us we were going on vacation, and then she put us all on this big, awful col-ored bus and there were photographers everywhere taking our picture…and then one time, one time at bear camp, she used me as bear bait in this really cheesy reality show called "Sarah Palin's Alaska.""

"I'm sorry, Piper, but I'm afraid our time is up for this week."

"YOU CANNOT SEE RUSSIA FROM OUR HOUSE!!! MY MOM'S A FUCKING IDIOT!!!"

"Alright, Piper, we're going to need to adjust your medication again..."

Trust me on this. I can see the future. And poor Sarah, she doesn't have one. Judging from her increasingly incomprehensible speeches.

Trust me on this. I can see the future. And poor Sarah, she doesn't have one.

In fact, judging from her increasingly incomprehensible speeches—if by "speeches," you mean a bunch of words and letters that don't go together and sound like a Right Wing Scrabble Board just exploded—even her most rabid supporters have thrown her under that multicolored Partridge Family Bus. As it turns out it *didn't* all come together when the hockey mom sang along...

As Sarah spirals downward into the abyss, her few remaining "fans" have become even more unhinged. They include a retired insurance man named "Sock" (No shit, that's his name) who saw me criticizing her on television and wrote me that he hopes "someone shoves an AK-47 up my hole and sends me off into eternity." He helpfully included his phone number in the letter. So I called him on the air and asked him, "What kind of real American would want to shove a *Russian-made* rifle up my glory hole?" And if he did, would Sarah Palin be able to see it from her house? Since it was technically a death threat, we sent the letter to the FBI, who helpfully advised me that my call to him was what they refer to in law enforcement circles as "unwise."

Whatever, J. Edgar. This is RADIO. No guts, no glory hole! In fact, I wanted to call my next book "I Probably

Shouldn't Write A Chapter About My Stalkers," but the FBI said no. *Again*. Fuckin' pussies.

YOU'VE GOT HATE MAIL

"I hope you get cunt cancer and die!"

This is only a sample of some of the loving missives Mama receives in her box every day. I divide my hate mail into two categories: people who can't find my box and people who feel the need to call it a name. In fact, I get called a cunt more before 6 AM than most people do all day. As a radio talk-show host for 30 years, I've had a long running conversation with the American people. Fortunately for me, I can hang up on them. Especially guys like "John from Amherst" who said the mortgage crisis was caused "by a room full of black guys." Or chain smoking "Road Flare Mary from Chicago" who once hacked up a phlegmy, "Show me a poor Jew." But my box has no protection. I can't stop what gets into it. Here's a sampling, organized by categories of crazy: sexist, racist, homophobic, violent, life threatening, just plain mean, and my personal favorite, all of the above plus grammatically incorrect.

Let's start with just mean:

```
From: Emily
Subject: You're a big idiot.
To: stephanie@stephaniemiller.com
Date: Wednesday, December 12, 2012, 7:06 PM


Shut your mouth.

~Emily
```

Then there's meaner:

```
From: Mdog
Subject: heard your drivel on FOX
To: stephanie@stephaniemiller.com
Date: Wednesday, December 12, 2012, 10:00 PM


just wanted to say you are a slimey socialist
biotch!!!
```

And then there's MEANEST (which, of course, also includes violent and life threatening):

```
From: the fish
Subject: chic fil a comment get a life
To: stephanie@stephaniemiller.com
Date: Tuesday, July 31, 2012, 9:27 AM


"LIBERALISM IS A MENTAL DISORDER" UNTIL YOU READ
THE BOOK WRITTEN BY MICHAEL SAVAGE, YOU WILL NOT
UNDERSTAND WHAT THEY ARE. CHRISTIANS HAVE BEEN
UNDER ATTACK FOR THOUSANDS OF YEARS. REMEMBER THE
ROMANS FEEDING THE CHRISTIANS TO THE LIONS. HERE
IS THE LINK WHERE YOU CAN READ UP ON LIBERALS-
```

THEY ARE TOTALLY INSANE. ORDER THE BOOK AND READ
IT MORE THAN ONCE, YOU WILL UNDERSTAND THAT YOU
ARE NOT DEALING WITH RATIONAL PEOPLE: THEY MUST
BE EXTERMINATED, THEY ARE A DISEASE TO THE HUMAN
RAC

You know what's a disease to the human "rac"? People who don't know that "race" is spelled with an "e"!

Then, as always, we have your garden-variety racist right-winger:

From: stephen
Subject:
To: stephanie@stephaniemiller.com
Date: Saturday, March 17, 2012, 6:14 PM

FUCK YOU AND FUCK YOUR MARXIST NIGGER OBAMA
Without exceptions, Marxists are enemies of the
United States Constitution
DEATH TO ALL MARXISTS! FOREIGN AND DOMESTIC!

As it turns out, racists often dabble in sexism too:

From: Bob
Subject: FOX NEWS VIEWER
To: stephanie@stephaniemiller.com
Date: Wednesday, December 12, 2012, 7:05 PM

This message is brought to you by a "White FOX
VIEWER. I might not be a genius but
I am white, and I am smart enough not listen to
your dried up CUNT… Have a good Christmas Bitch!

I thought it was a nice touch for a misogynist clansman to wish me a merry Christmas. I'm sure he meant a white Christmas. And P.S. Bob, my cunt's like Niagara Falls, just not for YOU pencil dick!

I'm sorry, was that sexist? Well maybe it's because I get letters like these:

```
From: Barry
Subject: Sean
To: stephanie@stephaniemiller.com
Date: Wednesday, December 12, 2012, 6:43 PM
Why are you angry, liberal woman always so damn
ugly? P.S. You are white like Sean asshole!
```

Or this:

```
From: Rob
Subject: Disease-infested liberal whore.
To: stephanie@stephaniemiller.com
Date: Tuesday, October 16, 2012, 5:26 PM

And that would be a compliment.
```

And how would my day be complete without the appropriate-for-any-occasion twat-o-gram:

```
From: Noah
Subject: You little TWAT
To: stephanie@stephaniemiller.com
Date: Wednesday, October 24, 2012, 6:44 PM

You little TWAT - go fuck off
```

And that's *before* I came out on the air as a lesbian. That's when the letters really started to get clever:

```
From: Salvatore
Subject: Not scared of any L words?
To: stephanie@stephaniemiller.com
Date: Wednesday, January 16, 2013, 8:25 AM

Lets see.
Labia licking lesbian from Lackawanna loser! :)
```

God, Tom Brokaw's gotten so *mean* since he retired. Sooooo sensitive about his problem pronouncing L's.

Then there was Stan, who first wrote in with a question:

```
Miller...How's America's favorite dumbass, lib-
eral dyke?
```

He was nice enough to write again though, and this time with a little encouragement:

```
Miller...What's up loser! Keep up the good work
lesbo...
```

Every now and then I get the whole trifecta: an exquisite mix of sexism, homophobia, *and* violence:

> From: Roger K
> Subject: Wow
> To: stephanie@stephaniemiller.com
> Date: Tuesday, October 16, 2012, 6:30 PM Stephanie
> Maybe you are just the sorry little bitch and
> stupid little fucking whore that you referred to
> in your broadcast. More like a stupid libtard
> lesbian with a penis envy complex. Get the fuck
> off the air you sorry ass. So how does it feel it
> get an Al Gore green fucking in the ass everyday?

Actually, that only happened when Gore sold Current to Al Jazeera for $500 million and I lost my job. Al, *call* me!

When they get super angry, they also get super specific—stage directions and everything. Like these next two gems:

> From: Richard
> Subject: treason
> To: stephanie@stephaniemiller.com
> Date: Monday, December 3, 2012, 10:57 AM
>
> you are a communist cunt and pigbitch. You are a
> LIAR and the same for that rat sitting next to
> you. The pendulum will swing some day, you better
> get your un-american bitch ass to china when it
> happens.

From: Robert
Subject: Hey Miller
To: stephanie@stephaniemiller.com
Date: Tuesday, November 8, 2011, 7:01 AM

Miller,
I got an idea for a conservative stunt. Why dont
we tie a chain to your big hips and drag you
around LA for a few hours? Wouldnt that be funny?
I think it would be hilarious. We could all watch
your fat ass going all around the city for a few
hours. What do you think about that Miller? Oh i
forgot, you're a dumb ass liberal, you cant think

Actually, I think the thing that hurt the most about that last one was the fat ass part. I go to spinning class or hiking every day and you can crack walnuts with my crack, you fucker. Check it out on Free Speech TV, 9 to Noon Eastern, check your local listings!

Lastly, here are my personal favorites—what Mama lovingly calls the "grammatically challenged":

Three faced liar morally emotionally bankrupt
polish slut William e miller lol would b proud
sarcasm someone who pitied you gave you a job you
broadcast your stench your whorish life hanging on to the legacy of your dead dad who lost
by the way I did like you But not anymore your
ugly it shows women like u and Hillary give ppl a
bad name of u must be gay jave some class I pity
u saaaad America is African-American not white

```
a damp shame indecisive loose michelle Malkin
anne coulter eat u for breakfast go Fuck yourself
miller bird brained crazy lost case
```

If u can debate me I doubt it call me when it done sucking bottles and old senators

And we end with the elegantly simple. This guy blew his whole load in the subject line before he even got into the "big box":

```
From: Jon
Subject: Dumb fukin broad
To: stephanie@stephaniemiller.com
Date: Wednesday, December 12, 2012, 7:01 PM
```

I may be dumb, Jon, but at least I know how to spell "fuck"...you DUMB FUCK!

THE END

P.S. If you think this is *actually* the end, just wait. Yes, it's true that MOST of my dreams have died. But I did get to finally meet Carol Burnett recently, and managed to babble: "I wanted to be *you*, but it didn't work out." The look of kind, empathetic, yet hard-to-conceal pity on her face reminded me of the look Pat Benatar once gave me when my friend forced her to watch a bad VHS video of me singing "I Need A Lover" with my radio station band in front of me. AND the look Barbra Streisand gave me when I shrieked in her face at a party: "Oh my God! You're Barbra Streisand! I love you!" AND the look on Oprah's face when I fell to my knees in front of her in mock prayer before she hissed: "Get UP!" You can read all about it in my next book, "How I Killed Oprah!" Ok, maybe not *her*, but one of her networks, and more about my career as the Typhoid Mary of television, killing off TV shows and networks willy-nilly! Fuck YOU, Fox Family Channel!!

But I do have one final dream left. And that is to be crushed to death by a whale penis. Like the unfortunate woman in a news story I covered on the show once, whose whale-watching boat got too close to a whale during mating season. Then I could have the "Chuckles the Clown" funeral I've always hoped for. "Dearly beloved, we are gathered here today because as you all know, Stephanie was crushed to death by a whale penis earlier this week..." Stifled giggles, rampant incontinence. My Mom: "Oh, dear." What better way for a comedian to go out than on a giant dick joke? Of course all of this will be in my last, posthumous book: "Moby Dicked Me."

Okay, if you know me at all—and by now we're BFF's—you're certainly not surprised that when I say "The End," I REALLY mean, "Oh, wait, I just have one more thing…"

I'm kind of like Columbo that way.

SOOO, here's the thing—if you had fun reading it, Mama would be eternally grateful (or at least until my A.D.D. kicks in) if you would post a review of this book on Amazon here. And if you feel the need to use the words "slut" or "pigbitch," you have my blessing. It's the thought that counts!

ACKNOWLEDGEMENTS

I would like to thank the man I stole from Rachel Maddow, political guru David Bender, for all his wit, wisdom, love, and help, particularly with the dead monkey funerals; my book agent, Gary Morris, for his patience and invaluable guidance in getting me ready for my close-up; my business partner, Ron Hartenbaum, or as my listeners know him, "the guy who owns the show who's trying to kill me for the life insurance money" for the fact that I'm not floating face down in my swimming pool; my "mooks," Chris Lavoie, Travis Bone, and Jim Ward, who rock my radio world and write all my fake fan mail. And finally, my friends John Fugelsang, Wanda Vonkleist, Linda Machenzie, Rob Reichman, Tricia Nickell, Craig Taylor, and Melissa Fitzgerald for always making me feel like Paramount is calling, no matter what.

Cover Photo Design by Ross Bigley. Thanks, Ross!!!

ABOUT STEPHANIE MILLER

(Photo credit: Danielle Levitt)

As the daughter of Congressman William Miller, Barry Goldwater's 1964 Republican presidential running mate, Stephanie Miller comes to the left, from the right. A frequent guest on TV programs hosted by everyone from Al Sharpton to Sean Hannity, Stephanie Miller is that special breed of liberal that even conservatives love because she's real... and wickedly funny.

Her national morning drive radio program, *The Stephanie Miller Show,* is heard by more than three million listeners weekly and she was ranked #12 on influential industry publication *Talkers* Magazine's "Heavy Hundred" list. *The Stephanie Miller Show* is also broadcast on Free Speech TV and has become one of the top-rated programs among that channel's thirty-seven million viewers.

Follow Stephanie at http://www.Stephanie Miller.com

on Facebook at www.facebook.com/stephaniemillershow

and on Twitter at https://twitter.com/SMShow

ALBUMS

The Best of Stephanie Miller's Happy Hour Vol. 1

the
FUNNIEST
+
the
FILTHIEST

from the
SM Happy Hour podcast!

Stephanie Miller's Sexy Liberal Comedy Tour, Vol 1

#1 BESTSELLING ALBUM

Best Tour
Best New Tour
Best Lead Comedy Performer
2012 POLLSTAR AWARD NOMINATIONS

DATE DUE

AUG 0 6 2015			
OCT 2 4 2016			
			PRINTED IN U.S.A.

CPSIA information can be obtained at www.ICGtesting.com
Printed in the USA
LVOW08s1612120716

496014LV00001B/110/P

9 781940 724065